This book is a must-read if you...

- want to explore new possibilities

- wish to discover your hidden depths and strengths

- are looking to expand your thinking

- would like to connect more deeply with the wisdom and way of water

- long to experience more joy, creativity and freedom

- want to let go of limitations and flow with the natural currents of life

- desire to make a difference through inspired environmental action

- are seeking to activate your intuition and inspiration

- are looking to access your calm, meditative Blue Mind

- wish to flow through challenges and change

- are looking to boost and build adaptive resilience

- crave to have the courage to step out of your comfort zone

- wish to live longer, happier and healthier

- want to be more like water, because you are WATER and water always finds a way.

PRAISE FOR UNCHARTED WATERS

All you have to do is look at this book's contents page to know you're in for a wonderful read. Author Julie Lewis uses all the many metaphors of water to share how we can dive into life, navigate its waves and wake-up calls, and flow through our days with awareness and appreciation.

These inspiring stories and insights will set up a ripple effect of positive change. Read it and reap.

Sam Horn
CEO of The Intrigue Agency

Uncharted Waters is beautifully written with a true honouring of the sacredness of water, sharing a wealth of information to awaken the memory that we live in an intricately connected universe where water is a precious life-source of living consciousness.

Through her deep understanding of the relationship we have with water, Julie takes you on a healing journey of discovery and inspiration. In reading her words, I could feel my own living waters coming to life."

Robbyne LaPlant
White Wolf Journeys

"Julie Lewis gently brings us down to the river and sits with us as we synch the flow of our hearts to the current. I didn't know how thirsty I was for this kind of water until I found Julie's spring melt wisdom."

John Roedel
Poet, Writer, Comic, Storyteller, terrible dancer

Uncharted Waters is a beautiful and moving journey of exploration of the self. Julie's insights and life lessons told through water remind us of the connection between nature, spirit and ourselves, and the value and vitality those experiences bring.

Katherine Rich
Founder of Rak Writers and author of *Nature Walk*

Throughout my life's journey, I have always been fascinated by the rite of passage that permeates our human odyssey. To exist with a sense of purpose and meaning without losing the richness of all our lived experiences on the road through the light and the dark.

Julie's Uncharted Waters odyssey is the epitome of a rite of passage as she takes her readers on a profound journey through the symbolic and physical attributes of water. Woven into the wisdom of each tributary is Julie's life path as she shares her most profound and often earth-shattering stories of loss, grief, resilience, strength, and the deeper message of her journey.

It was an absolute joy to share some part of this epic journey through our work together and as one of the beta readers. Julie writes with a wisdom that can only come from a deep dive into self and beyond.

The proof is in the delicate tapestry of multiple intelligences that are present in all chapters, and I promise you will never look at water in the same way again.

Mary-Rita McGuire
Transpersonal guide, and founder and gatekeeper of
MYSTERYM

As a passionate sailor and a business coach, Uncharted Waters: Discover Your Hidden Depths by Julie Lewis struck a deep chord within me. This book navigates the vast and often turbulent sea of personal and professional development with the deftness of a skilled sailor braving the uncharted waters.

Julie's use of water as a metaphor — from the resilience of the ocean to the adaptability of rivers — mirrors the essential qualities required in both sailing and business. Each chapter, with its unique focus on different aspects of water, resonates with profound lessons that are applicable to anyone navigating the complex waters of life and business.

As a sailor, I was captivated by the parallels drawn between the unpredictability of the sea and the uncertainties we face in our careers and personal lives. The book serves as a compass, guiding readers through challenges and encouraging them to embrace their journey, even when the destination is unknown.

For business coaches and leaders, this book is a treasure trove of insights. It encourages us to be like water — flexible yet strong, adapting to our environment while maintaining our essence. This perspective is invaluable in the ever-changing landscape of business, where the ability to flow with change determines success.

Uncharted Waters is more than a book; it's a navigational tool for life, urging readers to dive deep into their personal and professional quests. It's a testament to the power of resilience, adaptability, and the enduring wisdom that, like water, we must keep moving forward, no matter the obstacles in our path.

Mike Hoff
Founder and CEO of MHC (Mike Hoff Consulting)

The ability to adapt to change is the most important skill today's leader must explore deeply. In her latest masterpiece, Uncharted Waters, the incomparable Julie Lewis guides her reader with wisdom and experience that could only be shared by someone who's led over 60 expeditions and challenged herself to swim the English Channel.

Consider this medicine for the mind and heart, prescribed by someone who's struggled and suffered more setbacks than her abundant joy and optimism would ever reveal.

You'll glean insights not seen before, penned by someone who is a force for action and results. Uncharted Waters will give you the tools you need to face the future seeing all that's possible, no matter what waves of conflict you face."

Jeanne M. Stafford
Leadership advisor, Forbes contributor and speaker

Uncharted Waters is a transformative and thought-provoking workbook that navigates the depths of personal growth with insight and practical exercises. Julie's wisdom shines through each page, guiding readers on a journey of self-discovery and empowerment.

This book is a compass for those navigating life's challenges, offering a steady hand and a clear path toward positive change, which Julie so eloquently does on a daily basis.
A must-read for anyone ready to chart their course to a more fulfilling life.

Natalie Hore
Founder of Azraq, UAE marine conservation organisation, and Breathes Wellness, a mind-body organisation

UNCHARTED WATERS

Discover Your Hidden Depths

JULIE MILES LEWIS

Foreword by Dr. Brian Luke Seaward

First published in Great Britain in 2024
by Book Brilliance Publishing
265A Fir Tree Road, Epsom, Surrey, KT17 3LF
+44 (0)20 8641 5090
www.bookbrilliancepublishing.com
admin@bookbrilliancepublishing.com

A CIP catalogue record for this book
is available at the British Library.

ISBN 978-1-913770-83-9.

Typeset in Baskerville.

Bernadette Noll's *I Want to Age Like Sea Glass* is reproduced with the kind
permission of the author.

John Roedel's poems are reproduced with the kind permission of the author.

Mark Anthony's poem is reproduced with kind permission of the author.

The author and publisher have made all reasonable efforts to contact copyright
holders for permission and apologise for any omissions or errors in the form of
credits given. Corrections will be made to future printings if necessary.

For Laura,
Be Like Water
Keep Flame,

Julie. x

DEDICATION

For the Elixir of Life
WATER

With
Love and Gratitude

CONTENTS

FOREWATERED

DR. BRIAN LUKE SEAWARD, PH.D.

AS I TOOK MY PLACE IN the circle waiting for the session to begin, our speaker/facilitator, Doug Boyd, entered the room and took a spot in the circle next to me. Doug was the renowned author of the books *Rolling Thunder* and *Mad Bear*, each about a Native American Shaman healer. This session was an active guided meditation on the topic of water. After he sat down and got comfortable, Doug began to pass around paper cups. Then he turned to reach behind his chair, and grasped a decanter filled with water. He invited each of us to fill our cup half-full. As he did this, he began with a golden nugget of indigenous wisdom: *"Water is our first medicine."*

What followed was a powerful meditation exercise on the element of water:

To be aware of water from moisture in the air, to raindrops or snowflakes falling to the ground, to mighty rivers (the arteries of the planet), to underground streams and aquifers, to refreshing, clean water from the tap. Through his insightful guidance, we followed a stream of consciousness woven through with powerful, guided mental imagery to the cup of water we held in our hands.

We were then invited to place an intention of love and gratitude in the water, much like you would see if you placed a drop of coloured water from an eye dropper. The next suggestion was to take a slow sip of the water and as it passed over our tongue, allow the molecules of water to metaphorically bathe each cell in our body. He repeated the words: *"Water is our first medicine."* As we did this, we gave thanks to the gift of water and the long journey it took from the source to our bodies.

Like the cup of water we held in our hands that day, this book that you hold in your hand is a vessel containing timeless wisdom, colourful insights and powerful intentions to nourish and hydrate your mind, body and spirit. As you sip this wisdom, through the portal of your eyes, wrap the content in an intention of love and gratitude so that you may let these words permeate the deepest levels of your conscious mind.

It's no secret that at this point in the history of humanity, the topic of water has taken on tremendous importance. Droughts, floods, melting ice caps, sea level rise, desalination, dehydration, water contamination, ocean pollution, coral bleaching... the list is nearly endless.

As we enter into the age of Aquarius (the water-bearer), we are reminded that the element of water is a force to be reckoned with, respected and honoured. As such, may *Uncharted Waters* serve as a chalice from which to drink the refreshing wisdom that Julie has so masterfully gathered among these pages.

Uncharted Waters is more than an invitation to re-examine your relationship with water. It is a clarion call to action, so that everyone on Planet Earth may have unfettered access to this essential nutrient of life.

I am delighted to say that Julie has been a dear friend and colleague of mine for more than a decade. Over the years, I have had the great privilege of witnessing her remarkable journey as an inspiring writer, dynamic health advocate, authentic wisdom keeper, aquatic lover and fellow explorer of the remarkable human experience.

I raise a glass as a toast to Julie for an incredible job tapping the estuaries of wisdom so wonderfully in these pages, and sharing this wisdom with the world. Sláinte, Skol, Cheers.

Dr. Brian Luke Seaward, Ph.D.
Author of *Stand Like Mountain, Flow like Water*
Boulder, Colorado

Dr. Brian Luke Seaward is a well-known author, speaker and expert in the field of stress management and mind-body-spirit healing. He holds a Ph.D. in Holistic Stress Management from the University of Colorado, Boulder and has authored over 16 definitive books on topics ranging from stress management to spirituality and meditation. These include the bestsellers *Stressed is Desserts Spelled Backward* and *Quiet Mind, Fearless Heart*, and the acclaimed book *Stand Like Mountain, Flow Like Water: Reflections on Stress and Human Spirituality*. His wisdom can be found quoted in PBS specials, college lectures, medical seminars, boardroom meetings, church sermons, keynote addresses and graduation speeches all over the world. It has been said that he looks like James Taylor, dresses like Indiana Jones, and writes like Mark Twain! In the role of traveller, visionary, mystic, healer and mentor, Brian Luke Seaward has created a legacy in the field of wellness and health promotion for all to share.[1]

Artwork credit: Catherine Kay Greenup, Unsplash

"Stand like Mountain, Flow like Water." [2]
Lao Tzu (6th century – 5th century BCE),
Ancient Chinese philosopher

Introduction

Moving Mountains
to Uncharted Waters

DEAR READER: THERE ARE thousands of amazing books on the market, and you picked this one, so thank you! The book you now hold in your hands has been a white-water rafting ride with lots of unexpected twists and turns. Writing a book is hard, but not writing a book when you have so much to say, is also hard. The answer is to 'choose your hard'. My wish is that as you read through the book, you will experience a deeper connection to water and to yourself.

We live in such a complex, fast-paced world. Change is constant. It's imperative that reconnect with water's energy, wisdom and flow. Water, rather than oil and gold, is the new currency. Without water, there is no life. This fact alone makes it clear that we must take care of and respect it so it can take care of us as a species and future generations.

As you turn each page, you are invited on a thought-provoking journey. Each chapter offers the opportunity to dive deeper into the world of water, discovering its secrets, transformative power and healing abilities as the elixir of life.

Uncharted Waters has been a long time coming since my first book, *Moving Mountains: Discover the Mountain in You*, was published in 2016.[1] It's clear I had to experience many uncharted waters of my own, both professionally and personally, before this book could flow and finally come to print.

I thought writing a second book would be easy, having written and published one already. I was wrong! I quickly realised that my masculine yang mountain energy way was not the answer. The answer was to access my feminine yin energy of water, trusting it would lead me to new creative ways of expressing myself, all in good time, like a river flowing through many twists, turns and obstacles before reaching the ocean.

"Look deep into nature and then you will understand everything."
Albert Einstein (1879 – 1955), German-born theoretical physicist

MOVING MOUNTAINS

The stories, wisdom, and insights from leading 68 expeditions around the globe formed the basis of my first book, *Moving Mountains*. It encouraged readers to climb their own real and metaphorical mountains and, in doing so, build courage, confidence and resilience. The book was the cumulation of a series of wild adventures, experience-based wisdom and lessons learnt from more than 50 clients' stories.

My fascination and love of mountains began at the summit of Kota Kinabalu in Malaysia on 7th April 2002, my 40th birthday. I experienced a high-altitude epiphany to start my own expedition company that would give people the opportunity to connect with nature, challenge themselves and make a difference in the communities and countries they visited. It was a trip to Nepal leading a trek to Everest Base Camp in April 2003 that finally gave me the courage to take a leap of faith, resign from the security of a full-time job and start Mountain High, my own adventure travel business and the first female-led expedition company in Dubai. This leap was made easier with the support of an incredible human being, Jeanette Peck, who gave me the opportunity to operate as the Adventure division under her company at the time, Creative Travel Solutions.

Fifteen years later, I returned to climb Kota Kinabalu for my 55th birthday in search of another epiphany. This time, the message was clearly about water. It was pouring down with rain all the way to the summit, the paths were muddy, and several waterfalls cascaded from the mountainside. I was on a rock-solid mountain with water flowing everywhere. I felt the rain bouncing off my face and was reminded of the famous quote, *"Some people feel the rain, others just get wet"*. I was feeling the rain and felt as if the rain was trying to tell me something! That 'something' was to spend more time in, on and around water.

The weather on the mountain was a refreshing change. I interpreted it as a metaphorical cleansing of the old to make way for the new. For me, that new was a shift from the yang masculine energy of the mountains to the yin feminine energy of water. It led to me to explore what it was like to take on the hardest swim in the world known as the Everest of open-water swimming, the English Channel. More on this in later chapters. It's interesting to think that the mountain raindrops that I felt on my skin could well have become, through the water cycle, part of the same water (sea) that I swam in!

Over a period of many years, I've been thrown in or jumped in at the deep end with no other option than to be like water itself, flowing fearlessly through hefty and heartbreaking challenges that eventually gave way to calm waters and finally, the birth of this book.

The feedback from readers of my first book, *Moving Mountains*, was expansive and honest. One of the main themes of the feedback was, *"We want more of Julie, your pain, your feelings, your vulnerability and what you learnt as a result of all your life experiences."*

I remember recalling the words of Brené Brown, *"Vulnerability is not weakness; it's our greatest measure of courage."*

The beta readers for *Uncharted Waters* shared the same feedback with me: *"More of Julie, more of her feelings and vulnerability."* In this book, I decided to be more courageous and share more of me than ever before in good faith that it may help you along your journey.

THE INVITATION

When we look at life, business and our relationships through the element of water, without a doubt, there are many fascinating lessons to be learnt.

Entering uncharted waters is a metaphor to describe a situation where a person is facing an unfamiliar and potentially challenging situation, often where there is no path or precedent to follow. It's about embracing the journey into the unknown where the outcome is often uncertain. It's a metaphor often used in business, in particular relating to start-ups and entrepreneurs embarking on new ventures, requiring a high level of creativity and innovation.

On a personal level, it could be about taking on a new challenge, making a major life change, or facing a difficult situation with no apparent clear solution. It's an invitation to let go of the metaphorical anchors in our life, the limiting beliefs, fears and doubts that can sometimes keep us stuck in the harbour when we were born to break free, set sail and embrace a life of limitless potential. Setting sail is not always the best way to face up to our challenges. Sometimes it pays to stay close to them and focus on solutions from a grounded position of strength – in the safety of your harbour (your home ground). When this is the case, harbours offer a therapeutic and nurturing environment allowing us to recharge, gain perspective and find the strength to navigate through difficult times. Harbours are often peaceful and serene places, offering solitude and a calm environment for introspection and reflection. Whether you are seeking solace, looking for social support, or simply trying to find inspiration, harbours (your home) can provide a valuable respite during challenging periods in your life.

I am confident that new insights, approaches and solutions will flow as you learn more about water. I would love you to take this book as a timely and timeless reminder to believe in your dreams, discover more of yourself and create new blueprints for success. The biggest rewards come from being like water, that is, to have the courage to create your own path even when it feels scary and risky.

"Either you decide to stay in the shallow end of the pool, or you go out in the ocean."
Christopher Reeve (1952 – 2004), American actor and activist

Christopher Reeve was an actor, film director, author and activist, best known for playing the title character in the film *Superman* and three sequels. A tragic accident at the age of 42 left him paralysed for life. Rather than resign himself to the life of a quadriplegic, he actively campaigned to raise the profile of spinal cord injury victims and research.

I fully resonate with his quote because I have experienced the transition from the swimming pool to the ocean. In the pool, you have clear boundaries in the form of walls and the bottom; you feel safe and contained. When you venture into the ocean, there are no boundaries. No side walls to hang on to, no end to reach and, sometimes, no clear sight of the bottom. When we enter the ocean, a whole new world opens up; we discover more of ourselves as we discover more of the ocean and life below the ocean.

Navigating uncharted waters requires several traits and skills, some of the very same traits we ascribe to water: being strong, flexible, agile, adaptive, trusting, always finding a way. Like water, we must dare to move into new places and spaces, not fearing the darkness of the ocean depths.

From a health and well-being perspective, this book is a reminder to cleanse, detox and purify your thoughts and actions; to let the healing power of water flow through you and to you. To be more conscious, aware and appreciative of all the water in your life. The 70% water within you and the 70% that makes up our planet and gives life to everything. It's the mist, clouds, fog, rain, lakes, rivers, puddles, streams, waterfalls, icebergs, snowflakes, and oceans. It's H_2O and I LOVE it!

When we swim, water supports us; when we are thirsty, it is water that quenches our thirst. It's the most precious and critical component of life. With every drop we drink, and with every breath we take, we are connected to water. When we look at water, we are looking at a reflection of ourselves; read that again! **When we look at water, we are looking at a reflection of ourselves.** I say that because our body and the planet are made up of a whole ecosystem that depends on healthy water and air. Without them, we would die.

WHY ME?

Over the last four decades, my life path has taken me on a very diverse and often unusual journey, from the highest mountains to the deepest darkest waters. From the peaks of joy to the deep pain of grief. From Yorkshire to the Middle East. From employed to entrepreneur to primary caregiver. From homebird to a wild gypsy soul in search of new lands. From staying in five-star hotels to sleeping on shelves in a mountain hut in Iran. From feeling safe and protected to being held at gunpoint in the middle of the desert whilst escaping into Saudi Arabia because of the Gulf Crisis in Kuwait. From feeling totally alive to being in a life-threatening storm on a mountain in Russia. From speaking live on stage to speaking virtually from a self-created home studio. From having two amazing parents to saying goodbye to them both as they passed to the spirit world within two years of each other. From being widowed at 36 to being remarried at 45. These are a few of the uncharted waters I have encountered by choice or have had thrown upon me.

Who I am now and how I help others on their journey is a direct result of all these experiences. I have learnt so much about myself through the challenges, obstacles and turmoil I have faced. Through all these experiences, nature, in particular water, has been my saving grace. The ocean held me when I needed to be held. A long soak in a hot bath soothed me when I needed to be soothed. Cold showers re-energised me when I needed a boost. Seeing my reflection in a lake reinforced the importance of stillness, silence and solitude. Kayaking made it possible to see everything from a different perspective. Swimming gave me the opportunity to simply 'be and breathe' with the water.

Like water, I have managed to find a way out, over, through or around any obstacles in my path by responding swiftly to the environment I found myself in. Over the years, I have formulated a secret resilience recipe and a series of blueprints that have helped me flourish and flow through the calmest and stormiest of waters. I love sharing them through keynotes, workshops, retreats and expeditions. Join me to find out more; I would love to help you create your own blueprints for success.

WHY NOW?

Did you know that less than 1% of the Earth's water is readily accessible for human use? The vast majority is locked away in glaciers, ice caps and underground aquifers. This means that the water we rely on for drinking, agriculture, industry and sanitation is actually a very limited resource. That's WHY NOW we need to be even more aware of water and of the importance of taking care of it so it can take care of us. That's WHY NOW I needed to find a 'third place' and start writing to give water a VOICE and be that voice.

"Start writing, no matter what.
The water does not flow until the faucet is turned on."
Louis L'Amour (1908 – 1988), American author

MY THIRD PLACE

The concept of a third place for writers refers to a space that is neither home nor the office, but a creative, comfortable place and space where they can find inspiration. A 'home away from home' where it's possible to write, socialise, spend time in nature and see life through a new expanded lens. Sometimes it's a library, a park, a coffee shop or a co-working space. New people, sights and sounds to spark fresh ideas. For me, it was a house and dog-sitting opportunity in Cascais in Portugal in the summer of 2022.

The opportunity arose after one of my friends, Julie Buck, posted a note on her Expat Cascais Facebook group letting people know that I was happy to house and dog-sit for anyone taking a summer break. Within a couple of days, I was on a Zoom call with Leigh-Anne and her husband Chris to see if I was a good fit for what they needed. Thankfully I was and having seen their dog, a gorgeous cockapoo called Daisy, I couldn't wait to get there.

Quinta da Marinha was my third place for three glorious weeks. Daisy became my new best friend, walking buddy, joyful companion and curious observer as I laid out A4 sheets with notes and ideas for each chapter. My days were filled with early morning and late afternoon coastal walks, watching the ocean, looking for signs and messages from nature, sipping coffee, savouring Portuguese pastries, thinking of chapter content, and making copious notes.

Daisy and I became great buddies. It was hard to say goodbye when the family came back. Three weeks had flown by! Luck was on my side as a new third place opened for me making it possible to stay an extra ten days. This time an apartment sit in Monte Estoril and a new walking buddy, Alfie, an eight-year-old whippet.

During my time in Portugal, I averaged 25,000 steps daily. Living by the coast and having a dog is one of the best ways to stay fit and healthy. It helped get my mind, body and emotions moving again, and was perfect training for the Camino trip I was leading in early September. The time away from Dubai gave me the unique opportunity to reflect, refocus and soak up the healing energy of the Atlantic Ocean. Add to that the joy of spending time with Daisy and Alfie, getting to know lots of lovely people, exploring new places and having the freedom to write anytime and anywhere. It was the perfect recipe for creativity. Highly recommended!

WHAT DO PEOPLE NEED

Before I started writing this book, I asked myself, *"What do people need right now that wasn't as important as before?"* I sensed the need for direction, clarity and focus. For restoring mental and emotional well-being after a series of universal roller coaster rides, fuelled by a virus that totally changed the way we live, work, travel and school our children.

We needed a new map to take us to the undiscovered parts of ourselves that we had been too busy to explore in our *'always on and auto-pilot'* life. A map to help us break away from information overload, multiple distractions, technology and social media so we spend more time enjoying experiences with loved ones. Some people actually enjoyed this enforced pause whilst others suffered. Instead of doing what we had always done, it was a time to be more conscious, resourceful and creative; a time to find new ways of being, living, working and connecting.

During this time, one of my mantras was, *"When you can't do what you normally do, do what you can instead."* And one of my favourites quotes was, *"When fishermen can't go out to sea, they repair their nets."* We all had plenty of time to repair our metaphorical nets.

We had to turn fear into faith, doubt into trust, and frustration into patience. We had to listen to the quiet voice within, to trust our inner compass and adapt to the ever-changing external landscape. We needed to be more like WATER and find new ways to flow.

BE LIKE WATER

Experience has shown me that taking on the traits, spirit and attributes of various forms of water during different periods of my life, has helped me navigate the twists, turns, currents and tides of my business, life and relationships. My wish for this book is that it holds the potential to inspire, educate and motivate you to think more about water, to be more self-aware, to act and make positive changes in your own lives.

"Water is the driving force of all nature."
Leonardo Da Vinci (1452 – 1519), Italian Renaissance polymath

HOW TO MAKE THE MOST OF THIS BOOK

Uncharted Waters is a multimedia offering. You can dip in and out of the chapters, randomly open a page to read, or read the book from start to finish. The QR codes within the book link to images, sounds and guided exercises to help you along your journey. The intention is for the book to be an interactive and multisensory experience. You will find journal prompts interspersed within the chapter.

In addition, I suggest you buy a personal journal that you use in conjunction with this book. Make it your very own *Uncharted Waters* journal with plenty of white space to write, draw, or even paint the flow of your thoughts and ideas.

"Fill your paper with the breathings of your heart."
William Wordsworth (1710 – 1850), English Romantic poet

ROUTE MAP

In Chapter One, we explore water as the elixir of life, a source of health, healing and inspiration.

In Chapter Two, we discover the ways water can teach us some important lessons and how *'being more like water'* can help us in business and life.

In Chapter Three, we dive into water in motion, drawing analogies to the traits of tsunamis (wake-up calls), waterfalls and rain.

In Chapter Four, we explore how water creates change through tears, puddles and lakes.

In Chapter Five, we explore water's energy in the form of steam, streams and springs.

In Chapter Six, we go further and deeper to explore the flow and power of rivers, the sea and the ocean.

In Chapter Seven, we explore life beneath the waves and the lessons to be learnt from majestic whales and joyful dolphins.

In Chapter Eight, we explore water's unique presence in the form of icebergs and snowflakes, along with the revitalising power of fire and ice (hot and cold therapy).

In Chapter Nine, we dive deeper into the challenge, journey and transformation process, relating it to my attempt to swim the English Channel and the epic story of Mansour Al Dhaheri's Swim62 Abu Dhabi challenge.

In Chapter Ten, you will find anchoring rituals, oracles, symbols and signs to help you open up to answers from within and around you. They will help you stay calm, focused and grounded when you need to step back and take stock before you move forward.

Chapter Eleven is an opportunity to understand some of the key challenges we face when it comes to water and, more importantly, what we can do to be part of the solution rather than the cause.

At the end of each section, you will find three prompts to expand on the chapter content:

 Waves of Wisdom: three ideas – 'ah ha' moments – you had as a result of reading this chapter.

 Neptune's Trident: three actions you can take from reading this chapter.

 Positive ripples: find three people you can talk to about this chapter to create positive ripples.

TIPS TO HELP YOU FIND THE TREASURE WITHIN THE BOOK

1. Read actively, take notes, underline or highlight key words, quotes or passages. This will help you retain information and make it easier to find the parts that resonate with you.

2. You will find journal prompts throughout the chapters. You can skip them, dip into them, or take a break from reading, pick up your journal and pen, and fully immerse yourself in them. This is an interactive book. You get to choose how interactive you want to be when it comes to the journal prompts and rhetorical questions.

3. Keep a look out for themes: these can be found through the repetition of ideas, metaphors or examples.

4. Join a book club or start a reading group with friends to engage more deeply with the book and learn from others. At the end of the book, you will find a short section for book clubs.

It is said that we learn:

- ◆ 10% of what we read – read this book!
- ◆ 20% of what we hear – listen to water.
- ◆ 30% of what we see – look at water.
- ◆ 50% of what we see and hear – look at and listen to water.
- ◆ 70% of what we discuss – join a book club or join me on a retreat.
- ◆ 80% of what we experience – spend time in, on, around and under water.
- ◆ 95% of what we teach to others – share what you have learnt!

WATER QUESTIONS TO PONDER

Before getting started on the book, I invite you to find a space, ideally close to water, where you won't be disturbed for a while. Take a glass of water, a pen and your journal.

Get comfy. Close your eyes, relax your jaw, drop your shoulders, and take three deep breaths. You might like to have some instrumental background music playing while you do this. Stay grounded there for a while and when you feel called to do so, open your eyes then read the questions and prompts below.

Write whatever enters your head in your journal. You can come back to these questions at any time and make additional notes in your journal. It will be interesting to see if your answers change as you read through the book.

If water could speak, what would it say to you?

If you could be any form or body of water, what would you be and why?

(You might notice that the form of water you choose is exactly what you are seeking right now. The cleansing power of rain? The courage of a waterfall? The dynamic energy of a flowing river?)

Imagine what it's like to be a river, puddle, iceberg or waterfall! How does that make you feel? How does the form or body of water you chose sound if you were to translate it through your voice?

What emotions and words come to mind when you are in, on, under or around water?

How could being more like water serve you in your business, life and relationships?

What are you metaphorically thirsty for?

Which areas of your life do you feel drained, stagnant, or are experiencing resistance?

Which areas of your life are you experiencing the most flow right now?

If money and time were no object and it was impossible to fail, what soul-calling uncharted waters would you dare to venture into? (Move to a new country, change career, start your own business, commit to a relationship, sail off on an adventure?)

Have fun with this exercise and when you are ready to move on to Chapter One, turn the page and flow into the magic and mystery of your unlimited self through WATER.

WATER
IS
LIFE

CHAPTER ONE

WATER, THE HEALING ELIXIR OF LIFE

*"Thousands have lived without love,
not one without water."*

W.H. Auden (1907–1973), British-American poet and writer

IN THE SUMMER OF 2021, my mum was not doing too well. She was spending more time in bed, hardly eating, and sleeping a lot more than usual. I was in Greece when my sisters called to give me an update on how she was doing. It was clear that, sooner or later, she was going to be joining Dad who had passed two years prior. I jumped on a plane at the end of July and, along with my two sisters, stayed at home with Mum until she passed on 8th September. This was a precious yet challenging time for us all. I felt as if I was standing on the shore of a vast turbulent ocean watching the waves of her life crash against the rocks of mortality. Her once sparkling blue eyes started to become clouded with uncertainty and pain. Jane, Susan and I were caught in a powerful current of emotions, torn between the desire to ease Mum's suffering, and the profound sorrow of that the tide of life was pulling her away. First, she stopped eating, then she stopped drinking. She was living on air and the love we surrounded her with. She went without water for five days before she finally took her last breath: no water, no life. No air, no life.

I am sharing this poignant story to highlight the fragility and impermanence of life and the profound impact of water as a life-giving force. As water flows in a continuous cycle, so does life, with its inevitable endings and beginnings. It was the first time I truly thought about the impact of water on our lives. Water never dies; it changes form depending on the environment it finds itself in. It has no beginning and no end. Maybe we never truly die? Maybe we simply change form and ascend to the afterlife.

I know the above is a pretty heavy start to a chapter on water as the elixir of life. I also know that many of you reading this book will have experienced the loss of a loved one or will do at some point. Know that water is a powerful element and metaphor for the cycle of life, death and for healing.

Water is a sacred source of healing. Its physical and energetic properties are immense. In all sense of the word, it's an 'elixir' of life. Our deep affinity and relationship with water begins as a tiny embryo in a warm maternal human ocean. Eventually the waters break, our journey begins, and we take our first breath in a whole new world.

> "Water is the symbol of life. It is the symbol of purity, cleanliness, and clarity."
>
> Khalil Gibran (1883 –1931),
> Lebanese American writer and philosopher

INTENTION

When we choose to love and respect water, we are choosing to love and respect ourselves.

The intention of this chapter is to bring you closer to water, closer to yourself.

We drink water, wash in it, swim in it, sail on it and cook with it, yet it's fair to say that we often take it for granted. Water, like air, is a common element that most people don't pay any attention to; only when it's missing do we truly appreciate it. Without water, we can't survive. It sustains and nurtures all life on our planet; it's the only element that can exist in three forms: as a liquid, a solid, or as vapour. It can dissolve, transform, flow, cleanse and heal.

"Water is the first medicine of this world. Babies are born in water.
Water is life. That should be our first lesson.
We should never do anything to harm our water,
because if we do, we are harming ourselves.
Where did we lose this simple understanding?"

LaDonna Brave Bull Allard (1956–2021),
Lakota historian, water protector and
founder of the Sacred Stone Camp at Standing Rock

In his book *Water: For Health, for Healing, for Life: You're Not Sick, You're Thirsty!* Dr. Fereydoon Batmanghelidj[1] emphasises the importance of water in maintaining good health and preventing disease. Dehydration is the underlying cause of many health problems, including asthma, allergies, diabetes and hypertension. These lifestyle diseases can be managed and reversed through simple functional medicine practices, as simple as staying hydrated. The human body needs water to function properly. Most people don't drink enough water to meet their daily needs. Many of the symptoms of dehydration, such as headaches, dizziness or fatigue, are often mistaken for other health problems and treated with medicine when the body is not actually sick – it's simply crying out for water.

Water plays a vital role in brain function and cognitive performance. Even mild dehydration can lead to reduced concentration, impaired memory and decreased overall cognitive function.

Staying properly hydrated is essential for maintaining optimal brain health and supporting mental clarity. The brain is 90% water. Its function is directly impacted and influenced by the amount, quality and frequency of water that we drink. Knowing this makes it crystal clear that water is, indeed, the elixir of life.

Drinking water is essential to our health and well-being. It aids digestion by flushing out toxins and waste from the body. It boosts energy levels, reduces fatigue, is great for weight loss and regulates body temperature by allowing the body to sweat and cool down.

"Water is life and clean water means health."
Audrey Hepburn (1929–1993),
British actress and Goodwill Ambassador of UNICEF

Even mild dehydration can have negative effects on our body's ability to function properly. This can result in higher levels of fatigue, decreased reaction time and our overall ability to focus.

We need water to:

- Form saliva for digestion
- Keep mucosal membranes moist
- Allow body cells to grow, reproduce and survive
- Flush out body waste, mainly in urine
- Lubricate our joints
- Help the brain manufacture hormones and neurotransmitters
- Regulate body temperature (sweating and respiration)
- Act as a shock absorber for the brain and spinal cord
- Convert food needed for survival through digestion
- Help deliver oxygen throughout the body

"Pure water is the world's first and foremost medicine."
Slovakian Proverb

Feeling hungry, foggy-brained, not sleeping well and always tired? **DRINK MORE WATER** and eat more fruits and vegetables that are high in water content.

Stay hydrated by eating these 11 foods:

- Melons, such as watermelon, honeydew and cantaloupe
- Strawberries
- Pineapple
- Peaches
- Oranges
- Bell peppers
- Broccoli
- Celery
- Cucumber

The minute you feel thirsty, it's a sign that you are already dehydrated. Check your pee; if it's clear then you are doing well; if it's dark, it's time to rehydrate.

"Water is the lifeblood of the world.
Without it we wither and die."
Rumi (1207–1273), Iranian poet, scholar and mystic

START THE DAY WITH WATER

Upon waking, I drink a glass of water. It's a healthy way to start the day. Keeping a glass by your bedside makes it easy to wire this simple habit into your daily rituals. To help me stay on track, I have a very colourful one-litre water feeder that I take everywhere with me. It has time markers starting from 8am, along with embedded suggestions such as *"Get started!"*, *"Keep drinking,"* and *"Almost there!"*

As a 60th birthday gift to myself, I worked with a personal trainer to work on building more muscle and dropping body fat. Ana Monteiro, a Brazilian personal trainer, became my new best friend; a friend who pushed me hard in the gym and worked out a solid nutrition and hydration plan. I've always been good at hydrating, yet Ana challenged me to notch this up a level by drinking four litres daily (which is one litre more than I usually do). I did it by using the one-litre water feeder described above, filling it up four times per day. To spruce it up, I added berries, lemons, cinnamon, cucumber, effervescent vitamin C, or one of my new favourites, Humantra electrolyte mix.

I recently invested in a hydrogen water bottle. Molecular hydrogen is thought to act as an antioxidant, helping to neutralise harmful free radicals in the body, which reduces oxidative stress and inflammation, associated with aging and various chronic diseases. Hydrogen supports cellular function, and several of my colleagues, myself included, believe that it enhances endurance, reduces muscle fatigue and improves recovery by reducing the oxidative stress associated with exercise. It is also thought that hydrogen water might have some neuroprotective effects and potentially benefit conditions such as Alzheimer's and Parkinson's disease by reducing oxidative damage in the brain. It also has a positive impact on gut health by producing balanced gut microbiome and reducing inflammation in the digestive tract. More research is needed and, as with everything, individual responses to hydrogen water may vary.

Kangen Water[2] is a brand of alkaline water produced by a water ionizer machine, which offers various health benefits. Proponents suggest that maintaining a slightly alkaline body environment promotes overall heath by counteracting the acidity created by a modern diet. Due to the presence of molecular hydrogen (H_2), Kangen Water is marketed as having antioxidant properties. I am an advocate for Kangen Water and feel a big difference in my hydration levels and overall well-being when I drink it daily. Other benefits are improved digestions and improved skin health.

RECOMMENDED DAILY WATER (RDW)

We often hear talk about the recommended daily allowance (RDA) of supplements. I'd like to suggest we add in the recommended daily water (RDW). This would include how much water you drink each day and how much time you spend in, on or around water each day as part of your optimal well-being plan.

Wouldn't it be great if the health care profession started giving more nature-based prescriptions instead of the usual pharmaceuticals? Eight glasses of water, a daily walk on the beach, a swim in the sea, a soak in the bath, or an invigorating cold shower would be my prescription for anyone feeling anxious and low on energy. The key to longevity and good health is a combination of many factors. One of the key factors is super simple; it's **WATER**.

"Water is the only drink for a wise man."
Henry David Thoreau (1817–1862),
American essayist and philosopher

Gratitude is a huge part of my everyday life. When I drink water, I say thank you. When I swim in the sea, I say thank you. When I shower or take a bath, I say thank you. When it rains or snows, I say thank you. When I see a lake, river, stream, the ocean, a puddle, the sea or a waterfall, I say thank you. When I see huge glaciers and icebergs, I say WOW and thank you!

Make it a new habit to say 'thank you' every time you connect with water.

"If the only prayer you said in your whole life is 'thank you', that would suffice."

Meister Eckhart (1260–1328), German mystic and philosopher

DR. MASARU EMOTO

"Water carries within it our thoughts and prayers. As you yourself are water, no matter where you are, your prayers will be carried to the rest of the world."

Dr. Masaru Emoto (1943–2014),
Japanese spiritual scientist and author

There is no way I could write a book about water and not include the brilliant work of Japanese spiritual scientist, Dr. Masaru Emoto[3]. From his pioneering research, we can see that when water is exposed to such words as 'love' and 'gratitude' or beautiful music, it changes its molecular structure to form magical hexagons, crystalline works of art. When it's exposed to negative words such as 'hate', 'anger', 'fear', or heavy rock music, the crystals are misshapen and deformed.

Emoto's research involved exposing water to various stimuli, such as music, thoughts and words, and then freezing the water and examining its molecular structure under a microscope. He suggested that the molecular structure was impacted by the type of stimuli it was exposed to; that positive thoughts and emotions create beautiful and harmonious water crystals, while negative thoughts and emotions created disordered and chaotic water crystals.

Based on this research, it's fair to think that our thoughts, words and energy carry a vibration and frequency that have the power to impact us at a deep cellular level.

What we say, feel and do has a massive impact on the well-being of our internal waters. If you repeatedly say, *"I am sick and tired,"* then expect to become sick and tired. If you say, *"I am an ocean of energy,"* you will become an ocean of energy.

When you begin to realise that water has the capacity to memorise and transfer information, I am sure you will choose and speak your words more wisely.

> *"Your words hold great power. Use them with kindness and compassion, especially when talking to yourself."*
>
> Julie M. Lewis

Dr Catherine Clinton[4], author of *Structured Water Guide*, has discovered some fascinating research that adds to Emoto's theory that water treated with 'intentions' increased growth in human stem cells. Three Buddhist monks were given some water to look at and asked to 'hold intentions' that the water would increase human stem cell growth. Samples of mesenchymal stem cells were then taken from two donors and were used as culture mediums in both untreated and the intentionally treated water. The intentionally treated water showed an increased cell growth in the samples of stem cells when compared to the untreated water. Although this was a small study, its design and results warrants further research. Scan the QR code to learn more.

JOURNAL PROMPT

Start infusing your water with love and intentions.

What would you like more of? More love, more compassion, more energy, more abundance?

Draw a picture of a bottle and write what you would like more of on it.

Start infusing your water with your wishes.

Make water blessing labels to stick on your water bottle.

Place your water on a coaster or note with your wishes written on them.

I AM

What you write, you invite. Whatever you say after the words I AM, you become that word. I have a simple A–Z exercise that works a treat. Simply think of a word for each letter of the alphabet to describe yourself and repeat them to yourself often.

Here's a few ideas to get you started.

I am AMAZING.

I am BOLD.

I am COURAGEOUS.

I am DECISIVE.

I am ENTHUSIASTIC.

You can write them out onto slips of paper or keep them in a jar or small chest, and whenever you have moments of self-doubt, pick a handful out and say what's written on them out loud. Some people like to stick them on the fridge, the bathroom mirror, on their desk, or even tucked inside their wallet for easy access.

Emoto's work is a strong reminder to turn up our vibrational frequency and tap into what he refers to as the *"kotodama"* and *"hado"* of our thoughts, feelings and words; to be what he refers to as a *"Aikansha-bito"* – a beautiful human of love and gratitude.

KOTODAMA

Kotodama is a concept from Shintoism that states that words, either written or spoken, carry great spiritual power and can influence us and the world around us. The term is made up of two words, *"koto"* meaning "word" and *"dama"* meaning *"spirit"* or *"essence"*. In Japanese culture, kotodama is a powerful force that can be used for both positive and negative purposes. The sounds and vibrations of words have the power to influence the energy and vibrational frequency of the environment and can therefore have a profound impact on the physical, emotional and spiritual well-being of individuals and the world around them.

Kotodama is often used in traditional Japanese arts such as poetry and calligraphy. It is also associated with various forms of healing, meditation and spiritual development, where the power of words is used to promote healing and transformation in the individual.

The effectiveness of prayer, mantras and affirmations are prime examples. One of my daily mantras is, *"Every single cell in my body is vibrantly healthy."* It's one I asked my husband Calin to repeat several times daily during his journey from Stage 4 cancer to complete recovery.

HADO

The two words that make up the word Hado mean *"wave"* and *"move"*. The study of Hado tells us that the energetic vibrations from our thoughts affect our physical realities. Giving thanks for a meal before we eat changes the energy of our food, and the same applies to thanking water before we drink it.

One of the most important principles of Hado is to monitor your thoughts and intentions every day. When you change the way you speak about yourself, you can literally change your life. What you are not changing, you are choosing. Read that again. **What you are not changing, you are choosing.**

> *"Every single cell in your body is constantly listening to your thoughts. Make sure they are good ones."*
>
> Julie M. Lewis

BLUE MIND

> *"Being in, on or under water can make you happier, healthier, more connected, and better at what you do."*
>
> Dr. Wallace J. Nichols,
> American marine biologist, scientist and author of *Blue Mind*

"Blue Mind" is a term coined by Wallace J. Nichols[5], a marine biologist, to describe the emotional, physical and cognitive benefits of being in, on, around or under water. In his book *Blue Mind*, he explores the way in which water affects our mind and body, and how it can bring us better health, happiness and well-being. His research clearly shows that being near water reduces stress and anxiety, it calms our mind, and promotes relaxation and rejuvenation. This calm, meditative state is known as the "blue mind" state and is associated with a range of cognitive and emotional benefits, such as improved creativity, focus, mental clarity, increased feelings of connectedness, empathy, and compassion.

"Water quiets all the noise, all the distractions, and connects you to your own thoughts."
Dr. Wallace J. Nichols

His book shares the science behind this phenomenon, citing countless studies, research and stories of the people, places and activities that activate this state. In an *'always on'* and ever-changing world, our central nervous system can easily become frazzled.

Add poor nutritional choices, lack of sleep and hours of screen time, and you have a recipe for burn out. Disconnecting from technology and connecting to nature is the perfect antidote to our fatigued 'Red' mind. Our Red mind is present when we are stressed, anxious, busy, rushed or worried. WATER is the restorative solution to bring you back into your Blue mind.

In addition to the Blue Mind concept, the main theories suggested in the book relate to neuro-conservation based on the premise that nature and natural environments have a positive impact on mental health and well-being. Nichols suggests that by protecting and preserving rivers, lakes and oceans, we are not only protecting biodiversity, but also supporting human health and happiness. His work has significantly impacted the fields of environmental psychology, health and environmental policy. His research has led to the development of some great programs and initiatives including an annual 100-day #bluemindchallenge[6] that encourages participants to connect with water every day for 100 days in a row. It's a great way to make sure that however busy we get, we take time to connect with water and post a note on social media to share the blue love.

You can find out more about these initiatives under the resources and references section.

"You need the water, and the water needs you. I wish you water."
Dr. Wallace J. Nichols

BLUE LOVE & LIFESTYLE

Blue is my favourite colour, all shades of it. You will spot me a mile off because I wear a lot of blue. Even my eyeliner is blue!

I live and breathe a "Blue Mind lifestyle". Wherever I am in the world, I will find and connect with water. Most of my retreats and expeditions involve connecting to water, and living close to water is non-negotiable for me. Sitting on a deck with my morning coffee looking out to the ocean, picnics on the beach, and watching the sun set and rise are all some of my daily 'blue' rituals. My favourite blue love fix is a barefoot walk on the beach, then a meditation on the shoreline, followed by a swim in the sea. Blue gyms are good for the soul: think kayaking, surfing, water sports, diving, snorkelling, ice baths, cold showers, relaxing in a jacuzzi, or soaking in a hot bath.

Another one of my favourites is a floating meditation. I put my mask and snorkel on, lie face down in the sea, close my eyes, breathe, and let every single muscle in my body relax as I enjoy being held and supported by the water.

What's your favourite Blue Mind or gym activity?

"A drop of water, if it could write its own history,
would explain the universe to us."
Lucy Larcom (1824–1893), American author and teacher

BLUE ZONES & LONGEVITY

'Blue Zones' is a term coined by Dan Buettner[7], author and National Geographic Fellow, to describe geographic regions around the world where people live exceptionally healthy and long lives. He travelled around the globe and identified five Blue Zones: Okinawa, Japan; Sardinia, Italy; Nicoya, Costa Rica; Ikaria, Greece; and Loma Linda, California.

In these Blue Zones, people tend to live well into their nineties and hundreds, and are relatively free from chronic diseases such as heart disease, cancer and diabetes. This is attributed to a combination of factors including lifestyle, diet, purpose, exercise and social support.

Live to 100: Secrets of the Blue Zones[8] is an excellent four-episode series on Netflix presented by Dan. Over a period of seven years, he spent time in each of the blue zones to interview centenarians and learn their secrets to longevity. Through the interviews and inspiring stories, he highlights how these people have reached their golden years disease-free and remain mentally sharp. It's a must-see if you want to add years to your life and life to your years.

His book, *Blue Zones: Lessons for Living Longer from the People Who've Lived the Longest*[9], explores the common factors that contribute to their longevity. Along with the National Institute on Ageing and top researchers in the field, he uncovers nine factors for longevity.

These are:

- a plant-based diet
- strong social connections (finding your tribe)
- a sense of purpose
- regular physical activity

- making family a priority
- gardening
- faith
- a low-stress lifestyle
- and, for some, a 5pm glass of wine (grapes of life), enjoyed al fresco with friends and family.

It's interesting that finding your tribe and having the right people around you is the most powerful factor for a long, healthy and happy lifestyle. I am not surprised. Who you spend your time with has a massive impact on how you live your life. Choose your inner circle wisely.

Dan's book offers practical advice on how to adopt some of these habits, principles and meal recipes to increase your own chances of living longer, healthier and happier lives. The book, film and his website has inspired a movement aimed at creating more Blue Zones in different parts of the world and brings home the role of lifestyle and environment in determining human lifespan.

One of my favourite characters from the Blue Zones Netflix series is Jose Bonifacio, a 100-year-old cowboy who still rides his horse every morning! You will find Jose in Nicoya, Costa Rica. Jose has lived in the same house all his life, now with four generations of descendants, and openly professes his love of women and recites romantic poems. He looks super cool in his blue jeans, checked shirt and cowboy hat, and definitely has my vote for being a longevity legend!

Another of my favourites from the Blue Zones is Gregoris Tsahas from the Greek Island of Ikaria – where people forget to die! He's 100 years old and, aside from appendicitis, has never known a day of illness in his life. He looks a real character with his short-cropped white hair and ruggedly handsome face. He says he drinks two glasses of red wine every day (yet concedes he may have underestimated his consumption by a couple of glasses...). He's been married for 60 years and says the secret of a good marriage is never to return drunk to your wife! He's a regular at the café where he's known as a bit of a joker. He goes there twice a day and it's a 1 km walk from his house over sloping, uneven terrain. That's 4 hilly kilometres per day; I am sure many people half his age couldn't manage that!

ANSWERS FROM WATER

"They both listened silently to the water, which to them was not just water, but the voice of life, the voice of being, the voice of perpetual becoming."

Hermann Hesse (1877–1962), German-Swiss author, winner of the Nobel Prize for Literature

Water is such a wonderful reflecting mirror for our thoughts and feelings. When you are looking for answers, deeper wisdom or an overall energy boost, my advice is to look to WATER in all its various forms. Think about water, surround yourself with images of water, go to the beach, a river, or even sit by a water feature, wear blue, explore the emotions associated with different forms of water, and open the space for new ideas to flow.

TALKING TO WATER

Speaking to water and seeking guidance from it serves as a powerful meditative and reflective practice. It allows you to slow down, focus on your thoughts and engage in self-reflection. Personally, I find this very calming and centring. Water is associated with purity, cleaning, renewal and life itself, so seeking guidance from water is a way to invoke these symbolic qualities for personal growth and transformation. It's a natural stress buster, allowing you to vocalise your hopes, desires and intentions. I often sit by water and ask it, "*What would you like me to know?*" and wait for signs through the movement of the water. This is a fabulous way to connect more deeply with water and, in turn, connect more deeply with yourself and find your inner calm.

Be open-minded enough to consider new ideas and perspectives by looking at water.

- ♦ For courage, trust and freedom, I look to waterfalls.
- ♦ For reflective calm, I head to the lakes.
- ♦ For resilience, I look to the river.
- ♦ For connection, I head to the ocean.

What about you?

WATER AS A HEALER

During transitions, water is a great source of comfort and healing. It is used in many cultures for healing, ritual cleansing and spiritual purification. It's a symbol of life and fertility and is often associated with birth and rebirth. Water is used in baptism as a symbolic and ritual element in various religious traditions to signify purification, initiation and spiritual rebirth.

Scan the QR codes to listen to meditations from Dr. Brian Luke Seward.

Sacred water sites can be found all around the world and hold great cultural, spiritual and religious significance for various communities. Here's some well-known sacred water sites from different parts of the world.

THE GANGES

The Ganges River, also known as the Ganga, is a holy river flowing through India and Bangladesh. It's considered sacred by Hindus who believe that bathing in the river can wash away their sins. The river is believed to have healing properties, so much so that people travel to its banks to seek relief from ailments. The ashes of the deceased are often scattered in the river as it is thought that doing so will help the soul reach heaven. At 2,500 km, it is one of the longest rivers in the world, so in addition to its religious significance, it is also important for transportation, agriculture and supporting a wide range of wildlife and ecosystems. Sadly, it is heavily polluted due to industrial waste, sewage and agricultural run-off, meaning it is the exact opposite of its purpose and intent as a spiritual waterway. Efforts are being made to clean up the river through the enforcement of pollution regulations and wastewater treatment plants. However, this is a very slow and challenging process.

LOURDES

Perhaps one of the most well-known examples of the healing power of water is the town of Lourdes in France. In 1858, a young girl named Bernadette Soubirous claimed to have seen the Virgin Mary at the grotto of Massabielle in Lourdes. She was directed by the Virgin Mary to dig in the ground and water began to flow. Although there is no hard scientific evidence, many believe that the water from this spring has healing qualities and has cured a variety of illnesses and diseases. People believe the high mineral content of the water gives it miraculous powers and claim to have been healed after drinking it or bathing in it.

The most oft-quoted miracle related to Lourdes happened to Louis Bouriette, a 55-year-old man in 1858. Rendered blind in his right eye from a mine explosion (which cost his brother's life), Bouriette claimed that he immediately went to pray to "Our Lady of the Grotto." He washed his right eye in the Lourdes water repeatedly, praying for a cure. Suddenly, his vision returned completely, and in 1862, the cure was deemed "of supernatural character". A more recent case was in 2005. Delizia Cirolli had been diagnosed with a tumour on her knee. After drinking the water at Lourdes and praying, her tumour disappeared. Miracle and spontaneous remissions do happen; I know because Calin is a living example of it! (More on this miracle story later.)

ZAMZAM

Another example of healing water is Zamzam water located in Mecca, Saudi Arabia. Considered one of the holiest and most revered water sources in Islam, it has a unique taste and is believed to have medicinal, spiritual and powerful healing qualities.

Here are a few other sacred water sites you might wish to explore:

Jordan River, Middle East: The Jordan River is significant in Christianity as the place where Jesus was baptised by John the Baptist. Pilgrims come to this site for baptisms and religious ceremonies.

Lake Titicaca, Peru, and Bolivia: Lake Titicaca is revered by the indigenous people of the Andes. It is believed to be the birthplace of the sun god Inti and the moon goddess Mama Killa.

Lake Baikal, Siberia: Lake Baikal is the deepest freshwater lake in the world and holds deep spiritual significance for the indigenous

Buryat people. It is often associated with shamanism and local folklore.

River Nile, Egypt: The Nile was and still is vital to Egyptian civilisation and is associated with the goddess Hapi, the bringer of fertility and abundance.

Whanganui River, New Zealand: Known as the Whanganui River in Māori, this waterway has been granted legal personhood status. The river is considered a living ancestor and is central to the spiritual beliefs of the Whanganui iwi.

Uluru (Ayers Rock) Waterholes, Australia: Sacred waterholes around Uluru are essential in the beliefs and stories of the Anangu people and are considered places of great cultural and spiritual significance.

FIRST WORD

Helen Keller's first word, or more accurately, her first recognisable word was "water". Helen, who was deaf and blind from a very young age due to an illness, famously made this breakthrough when her teacher, Ann Sullivan, pumped water over one of Helen's hands while spelling out the word "water" in sign language on her other hand. This moment is depicted in the wonderful 1962 film, *The Miracle Worker*.[10]

A SOURCE OF INSPIRATION

Water is a source of inspiration for poets, authors, artists, business owners, CEOs and musicians, and certainly was for me during the process of writing this book! I had great fun finding watery places and spaces to write.

When I felt stuck, I took a swim in the sea to find my flow again.

When I felt drained, I took a cold shower. When I felt tired, I soaked in a hot bath.

When I was thirsty for new ideas, I drank water infused with the intention of creativity.

Whenever it rained, I took the opportunity to go outside and immersed myself in the rain.

Whenever I saw a lake, I took the opportunity to sit by it quietly observing my reflection and the reflections of the landscape. Whenever I saw a waterfall, I felt a rush and gush of courage, trust, and energy.

SHOWER POWER

Two of the beta readers on the book edit party I hosted, James Taylor and Alison Burns, talked about the 'shower power' effect, in terms of the ideas that flow when you have just woken up and are still in theta state. Theta brainwave activity is often associated with mental states that involve relaxation, creativity, daydreaming and deep meditation. It is a state that is neither fully awake nor fully asleep.

In theta state, there are no blocks to creative ideas. James speaks on creativity, innovation and artificial intelligence. I am guessing he gets a lot of ideas from his shower time and follow-up research. Alison is a renowned jazz singer who finds the shower an ideal place to warm up her voice and 'wake up'.

So, we can see that water is not simply a source of hydration but also a transformative symbol of hope, faith and healing. It's a precious resource which is exactly why we need to respect, protect and preserve it. It flows through our bodies, quenches our thirst, and sustains us in ways that we often take for granted.

The same water we use to make a cup of tea also forms the base of beer, wine and spirits. It comes in many forms and is the source of so much beauty and wonder. Its presence is needed in every corner of the earth. It outlives us all, it never dies, it keeps changing form to adopt to the environment it finds itself in. It can carve the land and shape our world to create stunning landscapes, rugged coastlines and a home for countless beings, corals, sea grass and glass. It can soothe, calm, refresh and renew our spirit.

I'll say it again: WATER MAKES EVERYTHING BETTER.

JOURNAL PROMPT

Before you move on to the next chapter, take out your journal and make a few notes:

 Waves of Wisdom: three ideas – 'ah ha' moments – you had as a result of reading this chapter.

 Neptune's Trident: three actions you can take from reading this chapter.

 Positive Ripples: find three people you can talk to about this chapter to create positive ripples.

In the next chapter, we explore how being more like water can help us in business and life.

BE
LIKE
WATER

CHAPTER TWO

LESSONS FROM WATER

"The water is your friend ... you don't have to fight with water,
just share the same spirit as the water, and it will help you move."
Aleksandr Popov, Russian Olympic swimmer

HOW EASY DO YOU FIND it to let go of the old and make way and space for something new?

How often have you let go, experienced something much better, and then wondered why you didn't do it earlier?

How often do you find yourself feeling stuck and stagnated?

Whenever I feel like this, I MOVE!

I walk, swim, go to the gym, do a few rounds of Wim Hof breathing, take a cold shower, shake up my routine, and reach out to colleagues for fresh ideas and different perspectives. Sooner or later, things start flowing again!

Scan the QR code to see Wim Hof's guided method breathing meditation.

Wim Hof[1], also known as The Iceman, is a Dutch motivational speaker and extreme athlete noted for his ability to withstand low temperatures. He previously held a Guinness World Record for swimming under ice and prolonged full-body contact with ice, and he holds a record for a barefoot half-marathon on ice and snow.

"Water does not resist. Water flows. When you plunge your hand into it, all you feel is a caress. Water is not a solid wall, it will not stop you. But water always goes where it wants to go, and nothing in the end can stand against it. Water is patient. Dripping water wears away stone. If you can't go through an obstacle, go around it. Water does."

Margaret Atwood, Canadian author, poet and literary critic, known for her prolific and influential contributions to contemporary literature

MOVE AND THE WAY WILL OPEN

One of the most important lessons water teaches us is to keep moving. When we move, we evolve and expand physically, mentally, emotionally and spiritually. Water itself is the perfect traveller, creating a path for itself as it does so, trusting that it is leading to something more expansive. Water cannot be contained. It refuses to stay in one form knowing that, within minutes, it can transform from a liquid, solid to a gas. Think about a waterfall cascading over the edge, trusting it will land and flow into a river, then on to the ocean with wild abandon, before evaporating into the skies, forming a cloud, and then returning as rain.

Water invites us to surrender to the flow of life and relinquish the need to control, knowing that whatever unfolds is meant to be. Most of the time, the need to control comes from fear. Fear of being alone, fear of failure, fear of missing out, fear of success, fear of letting go. One thing is for sure, you can't hold on to water, however tightly you grab it!

"To have faith is to trust yourself to the water. When you swim, you don't grab hold of water, because if you do you will sink and drown. Instead, you relax and float."
Alan Watts (1915–1973), British author and philosopher

LIFE IS ALWAYS IN MOTION

One of the key messages from Alan Watts' book, *Tao: The Watercourse Way*[2], is the importance of living in harmony with nature and the natural flow of life. The Tao (also spelt "Dao") is a central concept in Taoism (or Daoism), an ancient philosophical and religious tradition that originated in China. The term "Tao" itself can be translated as "the Way" or "the Path" and represents the fundamental principle that underlies and unites the universe. Taoism is often attributed to the legendary Chinese philosopher Lao Tzu, who is regarded as the author of the *Tao Te Ching*, a foundational text of Taoism.

The watercourse way refers to the natural flow of water and its ability to adapt and flow around obstacles. Watts suggests we can learn from the watercourse way by embracing the fluidity and adaptability of water in our own lives, to live in harmony with the Tao, the Way.

There are times to be still and times to move. Experiment with your own internal compass and intuition to guide you as to whether stillness or movement is needed. Stay still long enough to get more clarity, focus and direction, yet not too still that you fall asleep and lose momentum. Staying still for too long or moving all the time can either recharge you or drain you. After a few hours of white-water rafting, it's great to drift a while before being churned up again! After a period of stillness, it's good to move again. The goal is to be able to flip seamlessly between the two and know when to flip.

Being still is a great opportunity to gather our inner resources. We can use this time to reflect and review before acting. When you are sitting in stillness, looking at water can help you gain a deeper understanding of everything. It's a great tool for self-reflection and contemplation.

> *"Water teaches us to go with the flow. It can be gentle and inviting, or powerful and dangerous, but it always finds a way to move forward."*
> Yung Pueblo, American poet and meditator

INFINITY

During a Zen leadership training program with Dr. Ginny Whitelaw, author of *The Zen Leader* [3] and *Resonate* [4], we explored the infinity symbol as the time spent going inwards to reflect, review, reinvent, learn and grow, followed by time spent showing up in the world to share the lessons from the inward journey. The goal is to flow between the two. To continually learn, evolve, expand, integrate and share what you have learnt, then go inwards again for the next level of learning and awakening. The infinity symbol represents the interconnectedness and never-ending exchange of energy between our thoughts and our action. I love spending time alone to think about projects before sharing them with clients. I practice a healthy balance of solitude and social connection, of stillness and action, of silence and lively conversation. Weaving in and out of the infinity symbol.

FIVE WATER PRINCIPLES

I love Eastern philosophy. In my search for something to share here relating to water, I found some interesting information on a Japanese warrior named Kuroda Yoshitaka (1546–1604), who created five simple principles suggesting that the nature of water represents how man should live. They are:

1. The one who acts, makes others act; this is water.
2. The one who seeks his way and never stops; this is water.
3. The one who meets obstacles and multiplies his power; this is water.
4. The one who is pure and purifies those who are contaminated; this is water.
5. The one who fills the ocean, transforms to cloud, vanishes to fog, and freezes like a mirror but still retains his essential self in any form; this is water.

As a curious explorer, I relate to number two. I look for ways and don't stop until I have found them. If I can't find them, I find someone who can in the form of a coach, mentor or spiritual guide. I also resonate with number three as it relates to building resilience through meeting and overcoming obstacles.

JOURNAL PROMPT

Which one of the five principles of water do you resonate with the most and why?

Make notes in your journal about each one.

JOURNEY THROUGH LIFE

"We forget that the water cycle and life cycle are one."
Jacques Cousteau (1910–1997),
French oceanographer and filmmaker

The journey of water can be a mirror of our own journey through life. Water falls from the sky and begins its journey, shape-shifting to the different environments and conditions it finds itself in. We come into this life from a watery womb into an ocean of possibilities dependent on where we were born, our parents, our peers, our culture, our innate gifts, and our soul calling. We move through life encountering many twists and turns. When we live like water, we can move through life with grace, ease, determination and resilience.

Like water, we need to be willing to let go instead of clinging to the past, old ways, limiting beliefs, or fear of what's ahead. When a river breaks at a waterfall, it gains energy and moves on. Water inspires us not to become too rigid. Water is brave, it does not waster time clinging to the past; it flows freely onward and never looks back.

Like water, we need to be present and look forward because there's no going back in time.

Water does not run away from dark empty spaces. Like water, we need to be brave and flow into even the darkest or smallest of places and spaces, trusting they will lead us to brighter and more expansive landscapes. Water does not hold back from joining with a large body of water; it simply merges and contributes its energy without resistance or fear of losing its identity. Every time we move beyond our ego to become part of something bigger, we become more like water.

Water reminds us that even the smallest drop or change in temperature or environment can change its form and course. When we face changes, be they small or big, we need to choose to surrender and let go. The Zen expression *"Let go or be dragged"* springs to mind.

"You only lose what you cling to."
Buddha (480 – 400 BCE),
religious teacher and founder of Buddhism

If there's a better path to take, water always finds it.

If there's a better way to be, water becomes it.

If there's a better way to solve a situation, water solves it.

Be like water.

"Water is the most perfect traveller because when it travels,
it becomes the path itself."
Mehmet Murat ildan, Turkish writer and thinker

Many drops of water can create a lake and many baby steps taken can create the reality we dream of. Water reminds us that everything is in motion and that change, growth, challenges, twists and turns are all part of our growth and expansion. It teaches us to trust perfect timing and keep moving forward, despite potential obstacles ahead. Water goes wherever it wants to go and knows that over time it can wear away any rock.

"Be like water making its way through cracks. Do not be assertive, just adjust to the object, and you shall find a way around it or through it. ... Empty your mind, be formless. Shapeless, like water. If you put water into a cup, it becomes the cup. You put water into a bottle and it becomes the bottle. ... Be water, my friend."

Bruce Lee (1940–1973),
Hong Kong-American martial artist and actor

SHAPE-SHIFTING

"Moving, changing, flowing – that is what life is all about."
Dr. Masaru Emoto

Water is the only element that can shape-shift between three forms: from liquid, to solid, to vapour. It can find any crack or opening and use it to its advantage. It flows taking the path of least resistance to conserve precious energy. It changes form to match the environment it is in as it passes through the water cycle, much like we do as humans through our life cycle. It can squeeze through the smallest opening, it can evaporate into thin air, it boils, it freezes, and it takes the shape of the container it finds itself in. WATER IS AMAZING!

HUMAN SHAPE-SHIFTING

At the age of 11, I went to a Quaker school in West Yorkshire as a boarder. I was in a totally new environment, sharing a dormitory with strangers. I was away from my family and had to quickly adapt to this new way of life. In the first term, I struggled and missed my parents and siblings. There were many reverse charge calls to my dad for a pep talk. I spoke with a broad Yorkshire accent and everyone else seemed to speak so eloquently. It was clear I needed to shape-shift. Soon, my accent mellowed and morphed into a combination of several accents due to spending time with a very diverse group of students at the school. It took a little time to find my feet and immerse in boarding school life, yet by the third term, I was flourishing and often chose not to go home at weekends! Instead, I visited my friends' homes or joined hockey camps. In my final year, I was asked to take on the role of Head Girl and to this day my name is embossed in gold on a beautiful wooden plaque in the school vestibule.

Other examples of my shape-shifting include moving seven times in four years, changing careers in my forties and, more recently, for us all, having to adapt to lockdowns and totally new ways of living, being, traveling, working and schooling.

In both subtle and more dramatic ways, we can shape-shift by our choice of clothing, hairstyle and gestures to display a different persona and expression into the world. You will know when it's time to shape-shift. How? You will just know (and if you don't, maybe someone will tell you!) Have you been too long in one form? Are you feeling stiff and stagnant? Have you lost flexibility in your way of thinking? Are you feeling lethargic and longing for change? **LEARN TO SHAPE-SHIFT!**

ALL CHANGE

I think the analogy below by bestselling poet, John Roedel[5], says it all...

*"This isn't how I planned for
my life to look like," I whispered.
under my breath, as I walked to my car.*

"Tell me about it,"
an eavesdropping cloud
replied to me from above.

I looked up and watched.
the cloud billow between looking
like a dove and an open hand.

The cloud continued:

"I used to be a snowfield in Montana.
I used to be a dewdrop kiss on a lily.
I used to be a puddle in a parking lot.
I used to be a river in Mexico.
I used to be a glacier.
I used to be a waterfall mist in a jungle.

I used to be so many things."

"Doesn't that make you sad?" I asked the cloud.

"It used to — but not anymore," the cloud replied while wrapping herself
around me like a scarf. "I don't think either of us were created to stay the same
form our entire life."

"I'm not sure I can let go of my old life," I sighed.

"Oh, you simply must," the cloud whispered in my ear.

"Because once you release what you used to be
and embrace who you are meant to be now —
something amazing will happen," the cloud said.

"What's that?" I asked while looking at my hands that were beginning to
billow and shapeshift.

"You'll start to float."

and with that my feet lifted off the ground.

Printed with permission by John Roedel

JOURNAL PROMPT

What shape-shifting stories do you have to share?

What was the trigger for the change?

What did you learn about yourself through the change?

Think of a time you chose to let go, versus resisting and being dragged

I CHING - THE BOOK OF CHANGE

As mentioned, the Tao is the way of water. The *I Ching*[6], also known as *Book of Change*, is an ancient Chinese text that is often used as a guide to Taoism and the natural world. There are many key lessons and points about water from the *I Ching*. Here are a few of my favourites:

- Water is a powerful symbol for the flow of life and the cyclical nature of existence. By understanding the nature of water, we can gain insight into the larger patterns of the universe.

- Water is associated with the feminine in Chinese philosophy and as such represents such qualities and superpowers as receptivity, adaptability and intuition.

- Water can overcome obstacles through persistence and patience, gradually wearing away resistance over time.
- Water can transform itself and facilitate transformation in others.

K'AN

K'an is one of the eight trigrams used in the *I Ching*. It is associated with the water element and is represented by three solid lines stacked on top of each other. K'an is associated with the qualities of depth and stillness, as well as the emotion of fear and the potential for danger and uncertainty. On the flip side, it suggests the potential for transformation and renewal through facing our fears.

It is associated with the north and the winter season, emphasising the need for stillness and introspection during this time. The trigram also represents the qualities of flexibility and adaptability, emphasising the need to flow with the changing circumstances of life.

Water is such a powerful symbol for the flow of life and the need for adaptability in the face of change. By embodying the qualities of water and learning to flow with the changing circumstances of life, we can achieve a much greater sense of balance and harmony. By learning to flow like water, we can overcome obstacles and build real-time resilience.

The Way of Water is a concept found in many spiritual and cultural traditions suggesting that water has a unique energy and consciousness that can be experienced and learned from. The Way of Water emphasises the importance of flowing, adapting and responding to the changing circumstances of life. It's a concept that can be applied to many aspects of our lives, from relationships and business, to boosting our health, happiness, success and well-being.

Avatar: The Way of Water[7] is also one of my favourite movies. It is an epic 2022 American science fiction film co-produced and directed by James Cameron. The lines below from the film really resonate with me and fit in well with the theme of this book:

"The way of water has no beginning and no end. The sea is around you and in you. The sea is your home before your birth and after your death."

Avatar: The Way of Water, 2022 film by James Cameron

BUSINESS LESSONS FROM WATER

"The wise man is like water; he can adapt to any situation and flow with the currents of life."

Lao Tzu

Here are six business lessons from water that spring to mind, based on my 21 years as an entrepreneur.

ADAPTABILITY

Water is a great example of adaptability as it can take on different forms depending on the environment. In business, adaptability is a superpower as it allows organisations, teams and individuals to respond to changes in the market, new technologies and clients' needs. When I moved to Hong Kong in 2010, I had to adapt my business for a very different market. It was a time-poor market so people simply couldn't take a week off to join my expeditions around the globe. I had to start and offer shorter programs closer to home, do more speaking engagements and workshops.

RESILIENCE

Water can withstand extreme changes in temperature, pressure and other environmental factors, making it the perfect example of resilience. In business, resilience is critical to bounce forward, higher and stronger after setbacks and disappointments. It's the ability to stay calm, optimistic, flexible and manage stress. When I first started Mountain High in 2003, it took a couple of years to gather momentum in the form of cash flow and sponsors. My focused determination to succeed finally paid dividends in 2005 when I was sponsored by Land Rover Middle East with funding for projects and a brand new LR3 to drive!

COLLABORATION

Water is a key component of several interconnected ecosystems and sustains life. It teams up with the environment it finds itself in so it can give, receive or adapt accordingly. Collaboration in business is important as it enables organisations to work effectively with clients, stakeholders, suppliers and employees to achieve common goals. As a sole trader and freelancer, I make a conscious effort to collaborate with plenty of ground handlers and suppliers. I also team up with colleagues to deliver programs which gives me a healthy balance of doing my own thing and working with others.

INNOVATION

Water is a source of inspiration for many technological innovations, from hydroelectric power to desalination technologies. In business, innovation is critical to stay ahead of the competition, develop and improve new products and systems. When I started my business in 2003, my marketing was predominantly through speaking at different events and word of mouth. Over the years,

I had to get tech savvy and learn how to set up and manage a website, as well as a host of digital marketing tools to keep up with customer needs.

SUSTAINABILITY

Water is a finite source that needs to be protected and conserved. In business, sustainability is important to manage the negative impact of business activities on the environment and to create long-term value for clients, employees and stakeholders. I have teamed up with a marine conservation group here in the United Arab Emirates and have made a conscious effort to include regenerative aspects to my expeditions and retreats such as tree planting, beach clean ups and working with suppliers who have sustainability practices in place.

FLOW

In business, flow can represent the efficient movement of goods and services, as well as flow charts that allow for greater systems, productivity and quality. It can also link to the flow of ideas, inspiration and creativity. When I need new ideas to flow, I go for a long walk or swim. If that doesn't work, I get a bunch of my friends together to brainstorm new ideas.

By taking on these six traits of water, we can be more effective in business. These same six traits can be applied to start-ups and entrepreneurs. They can also be applied to relationships with the addition of communication, patience and trust.

In summary, here are a few key lessons from water for you to consider:

- Adapt to the environment you find yourself in
- Find a way
- Strength in gentleness
- Nurture yourself
- Be compassionate
- Be creative
- Be curious
- Be responsible
- Lead the way
- Be flexible
- Focus on your purpose
- Embrace change
- Find balance
- Stay calm under pressure
- Connect with others
- Embrace the unknown
- Weave around obstacles with ease and grace

- Recognise that every twist and turn is a new adventure with lessons that activate expansion and personal growth
- Water gives life to everything
- Don't force something to happen, let it happen
- Know that you are on your way to greater things
- Be unconcerned with the terrain
- Trust your path
- Be resilient
- Don't cling to things
- Give yourself the freedom to flourish and flow

"The knowledge of man is as the waters, some descending from above, and some springing from beneath; the one informed by the light of nature, the other inspired by divine revelation."
Francis Bacon (1561–1626), English philosopher and statesman

WATER AND EMOTIONS

After my husband passed in 1998, I went walkabout in Australia and found that writing about how I felt allowed me to slow down and reflect on the experience, instead of being in denial. It gave me the opportunity to explore my emotions in a more deliberate way, identify patterns in my thinking and gain greater clarity about what I was feeling and why.

Getting thoughts out of my head and feelings from my heart down on paper was very cathartic and allowed me to release emotions that were stuck at a deep cellular level. I kept a journal with me throughout the eight weeks I was there. I wrote when the feeling to do so arose, with no concern about grammar or punctuation. Most of the time I journaled when was in nature, on the beach, or in the mountains.

I think vast open spaces open our hearts and minds more; they remind us how minuscule we are in the big picture. The mountain becomes a molehill as we zoom out and see things from a very different perspective. Spending time in, on and around water was part of my healing process. It gave me a greater sense of connection with the natural world. Sitting by the water's edge, watching the ripples, or simply listening to the sound of flowing water, created a tranquil environment to help me process my emotions. Sometimes I would pick flowers and throw them on to the water as a symbolic *'letting go'*.

Writing about your thoughts and feelings is a powerful way to process your inner world. Whether you are dealing with a difficult situation, working through a problem, or looking to gain greater self-awareness, journaling is a valuable tool for exploring your thoughts and emotions.

JOURNAL PROMPT

Take time out with your journal to list the positive emotions you associate with water and the experiences that you had that evoked such emotions.

Note down any negative emotions you associate or have experienced around water.

What did you learn from these experiences?

Water is associated with a spectrum of emotions and feelings. The ones that spring to my mind are:

- Calmness
- Joy
- Wonder
- Fear

- Sadness
- Nostalgia
- Peace
- Fun

Water can be a calming influence that brings a sense of peace and tranquillity to our minds and bodies. It can evoke feelings of joy and happiness, particularly in the context of spending time at the beach with family or friends, swimming in the sea or kayaking, for example. It can also evoke fear and anxiety in people who have had negative experiences with water or have a fear of drowning.

After crossing the Drake Passage to get to Antarctica, I can vouch for the immense power of water to 'rock the boat'. I would love to have seen drone footage of our little blue ship bobbing along like a cork over and through the mighty waves. If you have ever been caught in a storm on open seas, you will know what I mean!

Kudos to the ship's captain for navigating us safely through a Force 11 storm. What a contrast (and relief) it was to reach the calm waters of the Antarctica Peninsula; now we had to navigate through the icebergs!

WATER IS:

Bold
Wise
Brave

Honest
Energy

Playful

Destructive

Adaptive
Intuitive

Calm
Disruptive

Powerful
Collaborative

Generous

Clean

Pure

Optimistic
Wet!

Refreshing

JOURNAL PROMPT

Before you move on to Chapter Three, take out your journal and jot down:

 Waves of Wisdom: three ideas – 'ah ha' moments – you had as a result of reading this chapter.

 Neptune's Trident: three actions you can take from reading this chapter.

 Positive ripples: find three people you can talk to about this chapter to create positive ripples.

In the next chapter, we dive into water in motion and draw analogies to the traits of tsunamis, waterfall and rain.

"Water never stops and says, 'Here I am. This is me.' It is forever in motion and twisting and turning into new forms every moment."

Laurence Galian, pianist, writer, lecturer, composer and teacher.

WATER
IN
MOTION

CHAPTER THREE

TSUNAMIS, WATERFALLS, RAIN
WAKE-UP CALLS - COURAGE & TRUST -
RENEWAL

"Nothing ever goes away until it teaches us what we need to know."
Pema Chödrön, American Tibetan-Buddhist and author

THIS CHAPTER IS AN invitation to explore how tsunamis, waterfalls and rain can bring our strengths, courage and renewal abilities to the surface of our awareness. They all have a significant impact on the environment and human lives.

Tsunamis can be destructive or transformative.

Rain can be life-giving or life-taking.

Waterfalls are a source of beauty, renewal and rejuvenation.

Over the years, I've experienced a few metaphorical tsunamis. The first one was during the Iraqi invasion of Kuwait in August 1990. I had been working in Kuwait for less than a year as the sports and recreation manager at the Holiday Inn Crowne Plaza. On the day of the invasion (2nd August 1990), I remember getting a call to my room asking me to come to the general manager's office for an executive meeting. Each of us were given specific responsibilities. Mine was to keep guests active in the health club and boost overall morale which, considering the circumstances, was a tall order for a 27-year-old who had no previous experience being in a war zone!

I set up squash, tennis and bowling tournaments along with extra workout classes. By mid-August some of the hotel's long-staying corporate guests had, through their company, worked out a way to escape across the desert into Saudi Arabia with a guide. Many of the women from this group came to my circuit training classes and offered me the chance to leave with them. At the time I had been advised by the British Embassy to stay put until a plan was in place to evacuate British citizens, so I declined the offer. Three weeks into the occupation, I was offered another chance to leave with a group of TNT employees from the hotel. There was no sign of things getting better and I had heard that certain nationalities were being rounded up from hotels and being taken to Baghdad as hostages...

I decided to take a chance with the group who had set up a plan to leave in a small convoy at 2am on 29th August. I let the executive assistant manager of the hotel know that I was going to leave and he gave me his blessing. I think he knew that I would be the first of many staff members to leave when given the chance. Times of choice are not easy times.

Leaving in the middle of the night was a hard decision to make as I knew it would be dangerous to make the crossing. Just the thought of it brought up fear of the unknown yet remaining at the hotel was no longer an option. I had to take a leap of faith, trusting that it would lead to freedom. I took one small bag with a change of clothes, my passport, water and some snacks. I wore a plain black Abaya (a robe-like dress) to hide my Western clothes, a Shayla (headscarf) to hide my blonde hair and dark glasses to hide my blue eyes. We were a convoy of six cars led by a guide who managed to get us off the main road and into the desert so we could cross into Saudi Arabia. It was a rough crossing. Our cars got stuck in the sand several times and we had to help each other out as best we could.

At one point, the lead car was stopped by a solitary soldier armed with a gun. I was in the third car in line in the convoy. I remember praying that the lead driver would be able to persuade the solider to let us all through. The soldier walked down the line looking into each car, gun in hand. *"Please keep walking,"* I prayed, hoping that he would not ask any of us to get out of the car. Luckily for all of us, he simply signalled to open the car window so he could see who and what was inside. After what seemed an eternity, we were waved on. My prayers had been answered. Thankfully, offerings of food and water from the lead vehicle to the soldier had been enough to secure our safe passage.

I can't remember how many hours it took us to reach Riyadh. All I remember was being very relieved to get to the Saudi border checkpoint where we were given a food packet and petrol voucher to refuel. We headed to the nearest petrol station then on to the nearest hotel to see if we could get a room for the night and make further travel plans from there. However, as a single female, it was not possible for me to stay at the hotel in Riyadh. I was taken to a refugee camp with the promise of getting an exemption certificate allowing me to join the rest of our group at the Sheraton Hotel where they had managed to get rooms for the night.

The exemption certificate never came; however, I was able to make a call to the British Embassy and request their help. Within an hour of being at the refugee camp, I was able to leave and go to the British Embassy. I called my parents from the Embassy to let them know where I was and that I was OK. They had not heard from me for three weeks so you can imagine their relief – my mum answered the phone and broke down in tears. Dad was in the garden and had no idea what was going on until she was able to hold back the tears and call him in.

Time was of the essence; we had a very practical conversation about getting me home. I didn't have a credit card or enough money at the time to purchase a ticket. I needed Dad to send funds as soon as possible to cover the cost of my flight back to the UK. The transfer was made and within 24 hours, I was on a Saudi Airlines flight home. It was a very emotional reunion at airport arrivals. I can only imagine how stressed I must have looked after such an ordeal. I ran into my dad's arms then pulled Mum in for a hug. Soon we were in the car and I was on my way home to the safety and calm of Yorkshire!

As soon as I got home, I called Holiday Inn Worldwide office in Brussels to let them know I had returned to England and would be happy to take on another post until it was safe to return to Kuwait. When it was clear the war wasn't going to end anytime soon, I also started to apply for posts in the UK. Within a few weeks, I was interviewed and selected for a post as Country Club Manager at an exclusive club in Wilmslow, Cheshire. This gave me a new focus and an opportunity to start rebuilding a new life for myself.

> *"No one can save us but ourselves. No one can and no one may.*
> *We ourselves must walk the path."*
>
> Buddha

The second tsunami hit me in 1998 when Hakim, my husband of seven years, dropped to the floor with a heart aneurysm and never got back up. Death of a loved one ranks the highest on the stress scale and when it's totally unexpected, I think it's even more of a shock to the system. Hakim was 41 at the time and had only been in Dubai for nine weeks when he passed. He was a professional squash player, and had played his last premier league match, winning 9-0/ 9-1 / 9-0 before collapsing.

Normally I would watch all his games but on this particular night, I had been held up at work. On the drive over to the club, I had a call from one of his teammates asking me if I was on my way, which I thought was a little strange. I pulled into the club car park, but it was busy and I had to drive around a couple of times before finding a space. I noticed there was an ambulance at the club entrance. Never in a million years did I expect that it was for Hakim. As I walked into the squash court area, I saw two paramedics on the ground using a defibrillator on one of the players. I froze in shock when I realised it was Hakim. I moved closer to let them know I was his wife. They tried everything to bring him back to life. Nothing worked. I sat beside Hakim, holding his hand until the police came. Still in shock, I called Caron Jones, the personal manager of the hotel where I was working, to let her know what had happened and asked what I needed to do next. Caron jumped in her car and came to the club to help me.

There were documents and reports to complete and sign and a request for me to go to the police morgue the following day to identify his body again and complete another round of paperwork. That night, I stayed over at Caron's. I called my parents to let them know what had happened. Dad instantly said they would book the next flight out to be with me. I was emotionally exhausted yet could not fall asleep. Instead, my mind was in overdrive about what this all meant. How on earth was I going to get through this?

The next few days were spent getting all the paperwork together to repatriate Hakim back to Egypt for his burial in the family tomb. Having my parents with me was a huge source of support. Twelve days after Hakim died, all the formalities were complete to take him back home. Now I had another round of challenges to face in terms of making sure everything was in place on the ground when I landed in Egypt. Hakim's squash colleagues in Cairo rallied round to help me. They were at the airport when I landed and took over all that needed to be done to release the casket and make the drive over to the burial ground. I was totally out of my comfort zone. If it wasn't for Hakim's English-speaking squash colleagues, I would not have had any idea of what to expect and what was expected of me. I could write a whole chapter on this experience and maybe I will in another book. For now, just know that this was one of the most emotionally challenging periods of my life. Dealing with a death abroad comes with many challenges. It made me realise more than ever the importance of having a strong support network.

Healing from this loss took time and a lot of soul-searching. Years later, I was able to turn the wound into wisdom and leverage the post-traumatic growth that came with it to climb my first mountain and start Mountain High.

The third tsunami came when my second husband, Calin, was diagnosed with stage four brain cancer in 2018. The thought of losing a second husband ran through my mind. I had to draw on my resilience and mental fitness training to switch my thoughts over to *"Let's focus on what we need to do and stay 'miracle-minded'."* More on this later in the book.

This trio of tsunamis was the greatest test of my resilience. I had to channel and manage all the inner resources I could muster and became an expert in managing my emotions and my energy to prevent emotional burnout.

"When you appear to have lost everything, you have nothing to lose."
Julie M. Lewis

Scan the QR code to learn more about Julie's story.

Wake-up calls can take many different forms. It could be a major health scare, such as a heart attack or a cancer diagnosis, that forces someone to completely re-evaluate their lifestyle, habits and way of life. It could be a financial crisis, such as losing a job, facing bankruptcy, or even a stock market crash that forces someone to take a more proactive approach to managing their money. It could be a personal crisis such as the end of a relationship, a marriage break up, or the loss of a loved one that forces someone to reassess everything. On a larger scale, it could be an environmental disaster such as an earthquake, wildfire or a hurricane that calls for communities and organisations to act and address the issues of climate change.

Wake-up calls force us to use two of the natural characteristics of WATER: **resilience** and **adaptability**. On the one hand, they can bring exciting new opportunities for growth and innovation. They open us up to discover new strengths and talents we never knew we had. On the other hand, they can be unsettling and disruptive, causing us to feel anxious, uncertain and overwhelmed. Often when we look back after something like this has passed, we can recall signs that foreshadowed it. We live life forwards yet understand it backwards by connecting the dots. Our setbacks become the set up for our comeback and, on reflection, they are often gifts in disguise.

"So often in life, things that you regard as an impediment turn out to be great, good fortune."
Ruth Bader Ginsburg (1933–2020),
American lawyer who served on the Supreme Court

It's only natural to seek shelter from storms and feel grateful when we are sheltered from them. In essence, storms remind us that we are not in charge of the natural world and cycles of life; we cannot control water's power, nor can we control the cycle of life.

HOW WATER HELPED ME THROUGH MY TSUNAMIS

Water gave me CLARITY. It supported me when I needed support, it energised me when I needed a boost and gave me answers when I took the time to ask for its guidance. As mentioned, YES – I talk to water, and it talks to me! I would simply sit by a body of water (mostly the sea), breathe deeply and consciously then ask, *"What's the best course of action for me to take right now?"* When the sea was calm, it asked me to be calm; when it was choppy, it asked me to take quick decisive action. Sometimes it would wash up a shell or rock to remind me of the gifts available to me.

During these challenges I needed to be more like water. This often meant letting go of control and surrendering to the flow, trusting that *'this too shall pass'*. Other times I needed to create waves and take decisive action rather than *'wait and see'*.

When I reflect on these times, I can remember weaving in and out of different bodies of water depending on what was happening. I am sharing them here as it may resonate with you and could help you on your journey.

Energetically I was a stream with a life of its own. Intuitively trusting and flowing.

Mentally I was an iceberg. Everything looked fine on the surface; however, there was a lot going on underneath!

Emotionally I was a lake. Still, silent, reflective. The slightest ripple would disrupt my peace of mind and I had to learn how to reset to serenity.

Physically I was a river, dynamically responding in real time to what was below and ahead of me.

Spiritually I was a waterfall, with the courage and trust to let go and go over the edge.

Socially I was an ocean, choosing who and what I needed to connect to for support.

I quickly learnt the importance of *'watering my own garden'* – that is, taking good care of myself and putting my mind and body first. To rest, restore and rejuvenate.

The type of wake-up calls I described earlier can be scary and make us fearful of how they might change our life and the life of those who depend on us. They require us to be resilient, resourceful and relinquish control; to be more like water, flowing fearlessly towards new possibilities that exist beyond the grasp of our normal functioning and imagination.

Wake-up calls can be exciting, transformative moments that bring about positive change, opportunities, and a whole new way of living, being and working. Many people stay where they are because it's comfortable. I know this because, in the past, I have done it. We stay because we don't know where else to go yet, or we are afraid to let go of the old to make way for the new. We live in the liminal space with one foot in the past and one foot in the future, knowing that to truly live a full and fulfilling life, both feet need to be striding into the future as we trailblaze a new path.

JOURNAL PROMPT

What wake-up calls (metaphorical tsunamis) have you faced in the last five years?

What did you learn from them?

How did you turn them into an opportunity?

GROWTH ZONES

*"If you realize that all things change,
there is nothing you will try to hold on to."*

Lao Tzu

The expression *"If it doesn't challenge you, it won't change you,"* invites us to take a courageous leap of faith and trust that we will land on our feet. The more comfortable we can be being uncomfortable, the more we can build real-time resilience, confidence and courage. I chose to move to the Middle East when I was 27. Everyone thought I was crazy and concerned as to how an athletic, blue-eyed, blonde sports scientist would integrate into life and work in Kuwait. I went with an open mind and spirit of adventure, knowing that if it didn't work out, at least I had given it my best shot. I was the first female Sports and Recreation Manager in Kuwait in 1989. It was a huge change from managing a fitness centre in Sheffield, as well as a steep learning curve that eventually evened out to the point where I felt totally at home, so much so that, despite the Gulf Crisis experience, I have now spent the last 23 years of my life in the Middle East, mainly in Dubai and Abu Dhabi.

"Not all storms come to disrupt your life;
some come to clear your path."

Paulo Coelho, Brazilian author

WILL WALKER'S STORMY STORY

In February 2023, I was asked to be one of the speakers at a Guinness World Record event for the World's Largest Safety Lesson in Abu Dhabi, as part of the Swim62 Abu Dhabi project. The safety lesson was delivered by Will Walker[1], the Founding Director of Storm Swimming Academy. He took the stage by storm (no pun intended!) and sailed through his talk to over 300 children and adults. Will tuned his tsunami experience into an opportunity to set up his own company, giving hundreds of children swimming lessons whilst schools were closed during lockdowns. He explained how he handled the Covid tsunami we all faced back in 2020. His story has the power to give anyone reading it the courage and drive to face their own challenges head-on and maybe even to welcome them.

I dropped into the Storm Swimming Academy offices in Abu Dhabi for a coffee with Will and his story is one I am sure you will enjoy.

"When Covid came along, I had a one-year-old son, my wife Emily was pregnant with our second child, and I lost my job as Swim Director for one of the largest academies here in Abu Dhabi. I remember sitting on my bed and crying for the first time in 10 years since living here. Money was so tight after losing my job that I couldn't even afford to buy a box of baby formula for my own son, which as a father was a very difficult time for me; a time I never want to go back to. I was 100,000 dirhams in debt on my credit card. I went to the labour court, and it was agreed I was dismissed arbitrarily so I received a sum of money to compensate for the massive loss of earnings.

All the schools and swimming pools were closed due to Covid and there was no chance of getting another job. Instead of paying off my credit card or buying other things we needed, I decided to invest in a trade licence to secure a visa for myself that gave me the opportunity to start teaching people how to swim in the comfort of their own private pools. I was soon teaching 150 children a week with a waiting list of 400 as all the academies and schools were closed! I figured the best way to handle this was to hire someone to help and took on a female teacher who became busy straight away. The demand for lessons was so high that I hired more teachers and over a two-year period, brought the team up to 42 staff – 38 coaches and 4 admin in the office – making us the largest swim provider in Abu Dhabi. At the time people thought I was crazy because there were so many restrictions on swimming and sports. I knew that a lot of great coaches had lost their jobs and were finding it hard to get a new one so I took the risk to hire as many as I could, trusting that the restrictions wouldn't last forever.

The name for my business, **Storm Swimming Academy,** *is a fitting name for the business that was formed out of a personal, professional and global storm. A storm is the worst type of weather I know. When I lost my job, couldn't feed my family and had no idea where my next income was going to come from, I was in the middle of a storm, a storm I never want to experience again. After a storm, the weather can only get better and thankfully for all of us it did. When I look at the Storm branding, I look at where I have come from and know that everything I do is aimed at making sure we don't ever have to go through this storm again. It's important for me that my family and all my coaches and their families are looked after. I feel proud to know that together we are teaching as many children as possible how to swim, to save their own lives and maybe go into swimming competitively, or as a coach or lifeguard and try out other water-related sports."*

It is said that we do things out of inspiration or desperation. I asked Will which of these was the driving force behind setting up Storm Swimming Academy:

"It was a combination of both. I was comfortable being an employee with all the benefits that come with it, yet I knew it was my dream and calling to start my own academy. Getting married and starting a family is not the best time to start your own business so I was happy to take the safe option of being employed. I knew I was more than capable of starting my own business, yet the timing needed to be right. Covid forced me to dive in at the deep end and start when the whole world was upside down. Knowing what I know now, I would do things differently. Asking for help and doing more research on how best to set up, for example. It's a lot of hard work, not the Instagram lifestyle you see! It's important to have a solid plan, and have people around you to work the plan and make suggestions on how to do things better. Having learnt so much from my own personal experience, I am more than happy to help anyone starting out as I genuinely believe in the power of helping each other out."

I asked Will, *"If water could speak, what would it say to you?"* and I loved his answer:

"I think water would tell me to slow down when I am running around to get to meetings and making big decisions. It would invite me to float on the water to calm me down then bring a powerful wave to get me back into positive decisive action."

When you face a huge wave of change, approach it with an open mind and a sense of curiosity. Instead of trying to control or resist the change that such a wave brings, focus on the opportunities that are emerging. Change is a natural and ongoing part of life, and our ability to adapt and navigate change is a key factor in our personal growth and success. The Serenity Prayer springs to mind.

In the early 1930s, Reinhold Niebuhr wrote the original version of the Serenity Prayer that reads:

O God and Heavenly Father,
Grant to us the serenity of mind to accept that which cannot be changed,
Courage to change that which can be changed,
And wisdom to know the one from the other,
Through Jesus Christ, our Lord, Amen.

What is clear from Will's story is that he chose to be the master of his fate rather than the victim. He had the courage to change that which could be changed. We can't always control the stormy waters and weather we find ourselves in; however, we can choose how to work with them. It was uncomfortable for him to be out of work with no sign of another job, a wife and family to support, and finances running at an all-time low, yet he focused on what he could do. He followed his passion to create what is now the biggest and most successful swimming academy in Abu Dhabi.

The master acts even though it's scary and the outcome is uncertain.

The victim blames, complains, justifies, and beats themselves up with negative internal self-talk.

> *"He who blames others has a long way to go on his journey.*
> *He who blames himself is halfway there.*
> *He who blames no one has arrived."*

Ancient Asian Proverb

Through various life experiences, I have learnt:

- That hanging on to the past serves no purpose.
- The importance of keeping your eyes on the path ahead.
- Not to look back over your shoulder; you are not going that way.

- To trust the path you are being taken on and have faith that it's leading to greater things.
- To live in the here and now.

> ## JOURNAL PROMPT
>
> What challenges have you purposely chosen recently? What unexpected challenges have chosen you?
>
> What are you learning about yourself through these challenges?
>
> Who can help you navigate these challenges?

THE BIG C

As I mentioned earlier, my husband Calin had a huge wake-up call back in 2018 when an MRI of his brain showed a life-threatening tumour on his left frontal cortex. Within 48 hours of the MRI, he was at the Cleveland Clinic in Abu Dhabi, having brain surgery. The surgery was successful; however, the tumour tissue removed was cancerous (stage four) so there was a huge after wave of treatment that involved radiotherapy, immunotherapy, cognitive therapy, and a lot of time in ICU and Ward 11!

During his treatment, Calin had kidney failure twice and was close to making an early transition to the spirit world at least four times that I know of. We both experienced a whole range of emotions: Calin as the patient, and me as the primary caregiver and patient advocate. There were so many practical, financial and logistical challenges to navigate. I became an expert on managing medical appointments, handling the insurance company and communicating with his oncologist, endocrinologist, kidney specialist and cognitive behavioural therapist. I got faster at *'fathoming the unfathomable'*. I continually strived to understand something that was initially difficult to grasp in terms of the time, energy and effort it would take to give Calin the best possible chance of pulling through.

The good news is that five years later, we can look at Calin's health wake-up call experience as a long *'pause button'*. For Calin, it was a second chance at life, finding more meaning and purpose through the experience, and moving forward with unshakable strength and resilience.

As Calin's primary caregiver, it was reinforcement that being more like water is a superpower and certainly one I mastered during this time! When a huge obstacle comes your way, a metaphorical or real mountain, you can take the hard route to climb or chisel through it; or you can take the path of least resistance and flow round it like WATER.

Caring for a stage four cancer patient is a full-time challenging job. During this time, it was equally important for me to take care of my own well-being to prevent burn out. The sea was my solace; it was the place I felt supported, where I could breathe, move, float, relax and let the saltwater wash away my worries. A daily swim, beach walk and grounding meditation in the afternoon when Calin was sleeping, was the 90 minutes that gave me the energy to go back to the hospital with a smile and be totally present. I was the *'bridge over troubled water'* providing comfort, support and reassurance that we could make it through this storm.

I have since spoken to many caregivers and the common stressors they all experience revolve around:

- Emotional stress
- Physical strain

- Financial worries
- Isolation
- Burnout

Having studied and certified in Stress Management with the Paramount Wellness Institute headed by Dr. Brian Luke Seaward, I was lucky to have a great selection of positive coping strategies and relaxation techniques I could tap into. Here are a few to help you:

- Asking for help
- Taking regular breaks
- Setting healthy boundaries
- Eating nutrient dense foods
- Staying hydrated
- Balancing solitude with social connection
- Sleeping well
- Breathwork
- Meditation to the sound of *"Om"*
- Listening to music
- Spending time in nature
- Swimming in the sea
- Reconnecting to all your senses
- Aromatherapy oils
- Barefoot beach walks to help you stay grounded
- Listening to the Solfeggio Frequencies[2] (powerful meditation sounds)
- Comic relief – making a conscious effort to smile and laugh
- Using and choosing your words wisely
- Having open and honest conversations with everyone involved
- Spend time in, on and around water

I can't emphasise enough how important it is to prioritise your own well-being so you can be present and more able to help the person going through the illness. For many people, the cancer journey begins with the shock of the diagnosis which is overwhelming. Throughout the journey, it's often an emotional roller coaster ride through fear, anxiety, sadness and anger, to moments of hope, resilience and strength.

Many women who have had cancer have told me that it's changed them in profound ways. Some develop a deeper appreciation for life and the people around them, while others feel a sense of loss or uncertainty about the future. Some become advocates for cancer research or patient support. Some say YES to the adventure of life. I know this for sure, as in 2012 I took 12 breast cancer survivors to Antarctica. Together they created modern-day history as the first and only team of breast cancer survivors from the UAE to make this journey. With the help of Astrid Van Der Knaap, our videographer and photographer, we were able to create a limited edition print run of a book in English and Arabic, titled *The Strength and Spirit of Women*, and a short documentary to highlight this inspirational journey. We only printed 100 copies of the book and all monies raised from sales of the book was donated to the Brest Friends Group.

FISH OUT OF WATER

The expression 'a fish out of water' refers to a person who feels out of place or uncomfortable in a particular situation or environment, much like a fish that is removed from water. It's a feeling of not belonging somewhere, such as going to a social event where you don't know anybody, starting a new job or moving country.

On the flip side, it is a huge opportunity for growth and learning, forcing us to adapt, learn new skills, ask better questions, and become more confident and self-assured. For me, it was going to boarding school at the age of 11.

This was my first big *fish out of water* experience. My junior school headmaster saw something in me and suggested I apply for a place at a private boarding school where he felt I would thrive. I remember sitting various entrance exams and wondering if I was smart enough to pass any of them (Yes, I had Imposter Syndrome at 11!).

Soon after, we received the news that I had been accepted at Ackworth, a Quaker school in Pontefract, West Yorkshire. My whole world was about to change. I would no longer be sharing a bedroom with my two sisters. No more jaunts across to my brother's bedroom to play. No more curling up with Mum and Dad on Sunday mornings.

As previously mentioned, I was leaving home at 11 to share a dormitory with complete strangers and experience a whole new way of life, away from my parents and siblings. I learnt to stand on my own two feet quickly. Slowly but surely, I adapted to this new way of life and stayed there until I was 18. This early experience of being away from home and getting to know and live with other students from around the globe was great resilience training for being an expat in the Middle East and Asia.

JOURNAL PROMPT

What experiences can you recall as a child or teenager that formed the foundation of who you are today?

What were some of the defining moments for you?

Did water feature in any of these moments? (Think learning how to swim, going on a boat for the first time, and so on.)

If so, how important / significant was it?

My experience at boarding school gave me the skills to navigate through university and my first overseas posting, to escape across the desert during the Gulf Crisis, to deal with grief when my husband passed, to climb my first mountain, start my own business, to lead trips around the globe, to attempt to swim the English Channel, and to speak on stage, to name a few! I purposely put myself in situations where the feeling of being a *'fish out of water'* is all part of the adventure. Doing this is a great way to keep you on your toes. It boosts your courage and confidence to be and do more; to go over the edge of comfort like a powerful waterfall, trusting that you will land and flow on to an ocean of new possibilities. It's OK to experience some discomfort when you try something new or are thrown in at the metaphorical deep end. Growing pains are a natural by-product of expanding and stretching yourself into new levels of possibility. Learn to trust yourself. Even if you feel unsettled, have faith that, like a waterfall, you will land, flow into a river and on to the ocean.

Speaking of waterfalls…

WATERFALL - COURAGE & TRUST

"Come to the edge," he said.
"We can't, we're afraid!" they responded.
"Come to the edge," he said.
"We can't, we will fall!" they responded.
"Come to the edge," he said.
And so, they came.
And he pushed them.
And they flew."

Guillaume Apollinaire (1880 – 1918),
French poet, playwright and short story writer

Waterfalls teach us many lessons that can be applied to our lives, both practically and spiritually. They teach us the power of perseverance and persistence in reaching our goals, even in the face of setbacks and obstacles. Their persistence and power wear down even the toughest rock formations and reshape the landscape, showing us that over time, we too can also break through and realise our dreams.

Waterfalls are constantly changing and evolving with the environment and water flow. They begin as one droplet of water joins forces with other droplets to form a fast-moving flow of water ready to cascade over the edge. This ability to change and evolve is useful for us as we experience new environments and embrace the changes they bring. Waterfalls flow with ease; they don't resist the flow or try to control it. Symbolically, this teaches us the importance of letting go; of letting things unfold naturally, trusting we will land in the right spot. Bungee jumpers, cliff divers and skydivers are like waterfalls as they take an exhilarating leap of faith.

"Throw your heart out in front of you and run ahead to catch it."
Arabic proverb

Every time I hear and see a waterfall, it literally takes my breath away. I love hearing them in the distance and then experiencing the joy of finding them! I love the sound of water gushing down the rock face over the edge, releasing a refreshing mist and spray as it cascades to the foot of the cliff. Scan the QR code to experience this beautiful sound for yourself.

Waterfalls are entrepreneurs.

Why?

Because entrepreneurs risk going over the edge every day!

As an entrepreneur, you encounter your own waterfalls every day. Sometimes the journey is smooth with a successful landing, and at other times you fall hard yet find the energy to keep moving on. In this sense, I think waterfalls encourage us to not be so rigid with fear. Waterfalls are brave and bold. They don't waste time; they never look back and have no fear of loss of control or identity. Instead, they gush into the vastness, willingly going over the edge, gathering energy and momentum with zero resistance! How powerful is that?

When I think of waterfalls, the following words spring to mind:

- Courage
- Trust
- Freedom
- Effortlessness

- Faith
- Energy
- Adrenaline

What words do you think of when you see a waterfall?

HUMAN WATERFALLS

Many years ago, I was invited to stay at the Ultimate Descents Lodge[3] in Nepal. One of the activities they are well known for is the 160m bungee jump over the Bhote Koshi River.

During my stay, I went canyoning, hiking and white-water rafting. When it came to the bungee jump, I remember looking over the edge to check the terrain below – rocks and a gushing river! I watched a couple of people jump and commented they were like *"human waterfalls"*! I decided I didn't want to be a human waterfall that day. My mental *"What if's"* were more powerful than *"Go for it"*. In my defence, I have done three tandem skydives for charity, jumped off the Macau Tower in China, rappelled down Wadi Mujib in Jordan, leapt off several rocks into the ocean, and love the wild rides you find at water parks – that's my kind of human waterfall experience!

> *"People may come, people may go, just as long as the water's slow.*
> *But watch out when you're headed for the waterfall."*
>
> *Waterfall*, Wendy & Lisa, from their 1987 album, *Waterfall*

JOURNAL PROMPT

What's the scariest thing you have done that involved courage and trust?

How did you feel before and after it?

What leaps of faith do you need to take in your business, life, relationships or health?

SPEAK TO ME

When I asked myself, *"If a waterfall could speak, what would it say?"* I came up with the following:

- ◆ Stop being afraid of what could go wrong; get excited about what will go right!
- ◆ Let your cares fall away.
- ◆ Make a splash.

- Be free!
- Share your energy!
- Be courageous.
- Trust perfect timing.
- Take a leap of faith and have faith.
- Remember you are water; you will always find a way.
- Make some noise.
- Keep moving.
- Live over the edge!

If a waterfall could speak, what would it say to you?

I think the Rumi quote below is something a waterfall might say too!

*"Don't worry if your life is turning upside down.
How do you know the side you are used to is better than the one to come?"*

Rumi

RAIN - RENEWAL

"Some people feel the rain, others just get wet."
Attributed to Bob Dylan, Bob Marley and Roger Miller

When it's pouring down with rain outside, what do you do? Stay inside, or run outside?

I love to run outside, holding my face up to the sky with my arms wide open because I find rain so refreshing. It's like having a deep power cleanse, a rejuvenating energetic bath of liquid light that washes away anything that no longer serves us.

Rain is a blessing from the heavens. It's liquid sunshine. A sign of renewal and growth, giving life to the tiniest of seeds and the mightiest of trees. I love how rain creates music of its own. It creates quirky new smells as it mixes with the earth. Everything flourishes and looks greener after a downpour.

NEGATIVE IONS

Have you ever noticed how much better you feel and sleep after a good thunderstorm? Going outside after the rain is good for your health; the air feels so much lighter because it's filled with negative ions. When you go out and inhale the ions, they enter your bloodstream and produce biochemical reactions that increase your serotonin levels. Negative ions generated by rain, waterfalls, ocean waves and thunderstorms accelerate our ability to absorb oxygen. Isn't it amazing that negative ions make you feel so positive?! Breathe them all in! My friend Alison can smell a thunderstorm coming and taste the electricity in her mouth. How connected is that?!

LESSONS FROM RAIN

Rain, like all forms of water, can teach us many lessons. I think the biggest lesson is the importance of renewal, recharging and rejuvenation. Rain washes away the old to make way for the new by flushing out stagnant energy. It teaches us the beauty of impermanence and the power of being able to let go of attachments, knowing that everything in life can change in the blink of an eye, much like a downpour that drenches everything, then moves on.

It teaches us the power of adaptability and flexibility in life and business, to be able to adjust to swift changes in circumstances or situations.

JOURNAL PROMPT

What other lessons can you think of from rain?

Reflect on your memories of rain – did it bring blessings or challenges?

Have there been times when you prayed for rain or prayed that it didn't rain?

If rain could speak, what would it say to you?

The American Buddhist teacher Tara Brach[4] has a RAIN meditation practice to help tackle difficult emotions when you are feeling overwhelmed. The practice helps to release you from the grip of the emotion so you can move forward with more ease.

R – Recognise
A – Allow
I – Investigate
N – Nurture

Scan the QR code to listen to Tara Brach's RAIN meditation practice.

RAINBOWS

Rainbows are created when sunlight is refracted through water droplets in the air. In many cultures, they are seen as rays of hope and the promise of good luck, or even a pot of gold! They represent a welcome sign that the storm has passed and better times lie ahead.

In many spiritual traditions, rainbows are seen as a divine intervention or message from the spiritual world to the physical world. I remember seeing a stunning double rainbow in Maui that looked as if it was connecting the sea to the sky. It was a bridge between Heaven and Earth, from the spiritual to the physical world.

After my mum's celebration of life, I returned to our family home and sat in the garden. I remember seeing a beautiful rainbow arc over the house. I like to believe it was Mum's way of letting us know that she was at peace and happy to be reunited with Dad. I also noticed several butterflies in the garden, so whenever I see rainbows or butterflies, I know Mum is saying hello.

Do you remember the double rainbow over Buckingham Palace on the passing of Queen Elizabeth II?

JOURNAL PROMPT

Reach for your *Uncharted Waters* journal and a pen, and make notes on this chapter based on the three pointers below:

 Waves of Wisdom: three ideas – 'ah ha' moments – you had as a result of reading this chapter.

 Neptune's Trident: three actions you can take from reading this chapter.

 Positive ripples: find three people you can talk to about this chapter to create positive ripples.

In the next chapter, we explore how water creates change through tears, puddles and lakes.

*"Heavy hearts, like heavy clouds
in the sky, are best relieved
by the letting go of a little water."*

Christopher Morley, American journalist and novelist

WATER
CREATES
CHANGE

CHAPTER FOUR

TEARS, PUDDLES, LAKES
LETTING GO - PLAYFULNESS -
REFLECTION

"Whatever the question, water is the answer."
Julie M. Lewis

AFTER THE DEATH OF a loved one, there are many tears. I know because I have cried rivers and I am sure you have too.

DAD

My father passed peacefully at home at the grand age of 95 in January 2019. Even though I lived the furthest away from home, I have always felt an incredible bond with him. I came home two to three times a year to spend time with my parents and siblings. These visits stopped when I was taking care of Calin as I had to channel all my energy into keeping him alive. My two sisters, Jane and Susan, were the primary caregivers for Mum and Dad. I took comfort in that they were in good hands.

I specifically remember speaking to Dad on 17ᵗʰ January. He asked me to promise that I would take care of Calin and told me he understood that it was hard for me to come to the UK right now. I let him know that I had asked Calin's sister to come over to Abu Dhabi from New York so I could take a break and fly back to the UK. I prayed that Dad could hang on until then.

Two days later, Jane called to let me know Dad had passed that morning. It felt like a sharp knife in my heart. Tears started gushing from my eyes like a wild river. In that moment, I felt that half of me had passed with him. I took a long walk on the beach until my tears stopped – it was a long walk. I walked into the sea, immersed my whole body under the water, then flipped onto my back to let the saltwater begin soothing and healing every single cell in my body. I spent so many happy days at the beach with Dad; I think that's why I automatically went to the beach after hearing the news of his passing. Floating in silence on my back, I closed my eyes and pretended he was right there holding my hand, floating beside me. He was – I could feel his energy.

Three days later, I was on a plane to the UK knowing that Calin would have his sister with him while I went to support Mum and my siblings. I made it home and was able to spend time at the Chapel of Rest with Dad. Seeing him in the casket was surreal. I kept expecting him to sit up and start talking to me. Instead, the conversation was one-sided as I told him how much I loved him. I recalled all the special times we'd shared together, the tears, the laughter, the joy, the moments of misunderstandings, the moments of clarity, and the things that had been left unsaid. I put my hand on his heart hoping that it would bring him back to life. I kissed his forehead hoping it would warm his cold and rigid body. I stayed with him a long time; I didn't want to leave. A river of tears poured out of my eyes and rolled down my cheeks. I know it's silly, but I thought Dad would never die. Maybe we all think this even though we know it's inevitable?

Months before Dad's passing, one of my friends, Anna, had given me a blue wooden heart with my name on it. I am not quite sure why I had brought it with me in my handbag. However, as I reached for more tissues, I felt it in my hand and instinctively brought it out and placed it in Dad's left chest pocket. It seemed a very symbolic and natural thing to do. My heart would be with him eternally. Heart to heart, ashes to ashes.

MUM

Two years later in 2021, I spent seven weeks with my sisters holding space for Mum as she made her transition to join Dad shortly before what would have been her 97th birthday. It was a precious yet heartbreaking time to see her spiralling into mortality, yet it gave us all time to spend 24/7 with her.

We shared pictures, stories, music, laughter and tears as we recalled our childhood years. We made a pact to make sure Mum's remaining days were as comfortable and peaceful as possible. Spending this time with my two sisters and Mum was very emotional yet very bonding; we needed each other now more than ever. I had felt remorse at not being able to spend more time with my dad before he passed; spending this time with Mum eased some of that pain. Knowing that they would soon be together again brought us all a sense of peace, but it also brought a sense of great loss. Once the mother ship goes down, it definitely feels like the end of an era.

The more you love, the more you grieve.

"Grief is the last act of love we give to our loved one.
Where there is deep grief, there is deep love.
Grief is a great rite of passage, it's a hero's journey of courage,
of sacred battles, sorrow, love, joy, and loss.
Through the darkness of grief,
we can see the light of love which transcends death.
And with the pain can come gratitude for the gift of the time we had,
the love that was shared and the power to become a better person
because they loved us."

Chaplin Robert Orr[1], Kindred Hospice, Nevada

Both of my parents passed peacefully at home, Dad in his favourite chair in the living room and Mum in her bed looking out to the garden. No dramas, no ambulances, no hospitals, just the simple sacredness of being at home. We all know that death is universal and at some point, we all experience the loss of our loved ones and eventually our own life.

As the late Queen Elizabeth II famously said, *"Nothing that can be said can begin to take away the anguish and the pain of these moments. Grief is the price we pay for love."* She was addressing the bereaved families of the victims of 9/11, but it can be used in any grief situation. It was widely reused on the death of her husband, Prince Philip.

TEARS - JOURNEY - JOURNAL

There's nothing like a good cry to clear the weight we are carrying in our heart. Tears are the physical, mental and emotional baggage we carry looking for a way out. Tears can be of joy, pride, sadness, laughter or relief. Over the years, tears have been the catalyst for many of my journeys and copious notes in a daily journal! I resonate with Brazilian novelist Paulo Coelho's quote, *"Tears are words that need to be written,"* [2] which is why I have several journals full of words.

First, there are tears, then time spent writing in a journal, then a journey. The journey can be an inward journey, a long walk, or a journey involving travel. Whether the tears are of joy, relief, pride or sadness, I still take time to write in my journal as it is such a powerful reflective experience.

Tears symbolise the ups and downs of life. As rivers flow and change over time, tears are a reminder of the ebb and flow of our emotions and experiences. Crying is one of the body's natural ways to release and process difficult emotions, as it activates the parasympathetic nervous system, helping us to relax and feel calmer. It also cleanses the eyes of irritants. Tears contain a natural antibacterial agent, lysozyme, that helps to prevent eye infections. When we cry, we can see more clearly – both literally and metaphorically.

Do you see tears as a sign of weakness and vulnerability, or a powerful expression of our humanity and resilience?

"Tears come from the heart, not from the brain."
Leonardo da Vinci

I agree with Leonardo. The kind of tears when we grieve the loss of a loved one are the ones that come straight from a pure-feeling heart rather than a thinking brain.

"Tears are the safety valve of the heart when too much pressure is laid on it."
Albert Richard Smith (1816 – 1860),
English author and mountaineer

When tears stop flowing, I find it useful to think about and honour your loved one's spirit by reflecting on the things you loved most about them, knowing that part of them lives on through you. My dad's love of learning, walking, travelling and his entrepreneurial spirit continue to flow through me. My mum's sense of humour, caring spirit and love of family flow through me; however, I still can't make Yorkshire puddings like she did! I am a soup, salad, smoothies and stir fry kinda girl!

Tears often flow when you least expect them as I found out. I attended a Gladiator Mastery program run by Dariush Soudi[3] in Dubai, when my emotions were still raw from grieving my parents' passing.

One of the exercises in the program was to write a letter to your future self. Within minutes of the exercise, I was overwhelmed by a flood of tears triggered by the music playing in the background. It was *Dance with My Father*[4] by Luther Vandross. Google the lyrics and watch the video on YouTube[5] – it is a beautiful, poignant song that works on so many levels.

Memories came flooding back of the times I watched my parents dance together with so much love in their eyes. Dad taught me and my two sisters how to waltz, cha cha cha and foxtrot, so that when we went to gala dinners with him, we could be confident on the dance floor. The first dance was always with Mum, then Jane, then Susan, and finally me, the youngest of the girls. Dancing with my father made me feel so connected to him. I felt like a princess being guided and swirled around the dance floor by the man, who, along with my mother, had given me the greatest gift; the gift of life.

I cried for a good ten minutes before using my tears to inspire words on paper. I calmed myself through an internal conversation. *"I feel this way and I am crying because I miss my parents so much. I miss dancing with my father. I miss talking, laughing, eating and simply being around them. I'm sad they won't see my future self; they won't see me doing some of things that I know would make them so proud."* This short internal awareness conversation brought me clarity and calm. Going inwards is a powerful tool. Be an inner explorer!

JOURNAL PROMPT

What soundtracks trigger your tears?

Recollect the times you have cried tears of:

- Joy
- Pride
- Laughter
- Sadness
- Grief
- Relief
- Frustration

From peeling an onion!

Who or what triggered the tears?

Were you alone or was someone with you?

EMOTIONS IN MOTION

I cried with joy and elation on reaching the summit of my first mountain to mark my 40th birthday back in 2002. I cried with relief when Calin's MRI and PET scans were clear. I cried tears of disappointment after being pulled out of the English Channel only four hours into the swim. I cried tears of frustration and exhaustion after being caught in a mountain storm that prevented Calin and me reaching the summit of Mount Elbrus in Russia. A year later on the same mountain, I cried tears of joy as we reached the summit.

I had watery eyes of pride when I met and shook hands with the ruler of the UAE, H.H Sheikh Mohamed bin Zayed Al Nahyan, in recognition of supporting the Swim62 project that you will read more about in Chapter 9. Tears of awe and wonder have trickled down my face when listening to monks chanting in Nepal, Tibet and Bhutan. After walking the last 111 km of the Camino de Santiago, it was the divine voice of a nun singing in Santiago Cathedral that brought tears to my eyes. As you might have already gathered, despite being known as the Queen of Resilience, I am also human and tears are one of many ways to connect with my humanness.

Have you ever wondered if there is a difference in the chemical composition of tears of joy and tears of sadness? Well, there is! Tears of joy contain more endorphins which are natural painkillers and mood boosters. Endorphins are released the minute we smile, laugh, exercise or feel joy in response to a positive stimulus.

Tears of sadness contain higher levels of cortisol which is a stress hormone released in response to sadness, anxiety or fear. Tears of sadness also contain more protein-based hormones and chemicals, such as prolactin and adrenocorticotropic hormone (ACTH) which are not present in tears of joy.

Whatever the stimulus is for tears, they all contain salt and water.

> *"The cure for anything is salt water, sweat, tears or the sea."*
> Isak Dinesen, pen name of Karen Blixen (1885 –1962),
> Danish author

Tears and crying are very powerful symbols in many cultures and religions around the world. In some native American cultures, it is believed that crying is a way to purify the soul and release negative energy. In some African cultures, crying honours the dead and helps release the spirits of the departed so they can move on to the afterlife. In Greek mythology, Aphrodite cried tears of blood when her lover Adonis died. The flowers that grew where her tears fell turned into red roses.

In Chinese mythology, the goddess Nuwa created humans by shaping clay then crying tears of sadness over them. Her tears gave humans their souls and emotions. In Christian tradition, there are countless stories of statues and paintings of the Virgin Mary that are said to weep tears of blood. This phenomenon is often interpreted as a sign of impending disaster or divine intervention.

According to Greek mythology, the phoenix was a mythical bird that would die and be reborn from its own ashes. Its tears were said to have healing powers that could bring about new life and growth. The tears of the Egyptian Goddess Isis were tears of gold that had the power to heal and bring about prosperity.

In Japanese mythology, the statue of Jizo is a Buddhist deity who brings comfort to those suffering. It is said that if someone who has committed a sin weeps before the statue, their tears will wash away their guilt.

Clearly, tears have been a powerful symbol of spirituality and human emotion throughout history.

In Japan, "rui-katsu" classes are offered which translates as "tear-seeking". These are regular crying sessions, which provide a safe space for people to process their more difficult emotions. Even tears of joy can be purifying and can uplift the spirit. When you next cry, remember that it takes a truly strong person to be vulnerable in our modern world.

Toxic masculinity is a harmful cultural norm that associates traditional male traits with emotional suppression and toughness. The phrase *"men don't cry"* epitomises this aspect of toxic masculinity, reinforcing the idea that men should not openly express vulnerability or sadness. This expectation can have damaging consequences, as it discourages emotional authenticity and denies men the opportunity to process their feelings in a healthy way. It perpetuates a limited and unhealthy notion of masculinity, which can lead to repressed emotions, mental health issues, and difficulties in forming meaningful relationships. Challenging these stereotypes and promoting emotional expression and vulnerability is essential for breaking free from toxic masculinity's harmful grip and fostering healthier attitudes toward masculinity and emotional well-being.

"Cry, forgive, learn, move on.
Let the tears water the seeds of your future happiness."

Steve Maraboli, speaker, bestselling author and behavioural science academic

AUDREY

Acknowledging and expressing our emotions leads to greater emotional resilience and well-being. In my first book, *Moving Mountains, Discover the Mountain in You*, I shared the A.U.D.R.E.Y. principle. So many people said it helped them so I'm sharing it here again. Whether we are aware of it or not, we are continually contributing to our life story by how we think, act, feel and speak. This includes our internal dialogue which can either make us or break us. If you were to say out loud the self-talk in your head, I think you might be surprised by what you say to yourself! Is it empowering or disempowering?

The concept of AUDREY is that as soon as you become aware of your self-talk, then start to understand it, you can disassociate from it and re-script and reprogram it to positive self-talk and an empowering emotional state to create your YES.

A = Awareness
U = Understanding
D = Disassociation
R = Reprogram & Re-script
E = Emotionally charged
Y = YES!

It's an easy acronym to remember and as simple as it is, it's a great self-regulating tool. As this book is about water, I came up with an acronym for water. Water carries so much wisdom that we can tap into. It has the power to activate and transform our biology and environment. It's liquid energy and it's very resilient!

W = Wisdom
A = Activation
T = Transformation
E = Energy
R = Resilience

WHO WILL CRY WHEN YOU DIE?

"But a mermaid has no tears, therefore she suffers so much more."
Hans Christian Andersen (1805 – 1875),
Danish writer of fairy tales

One of my friends, Isobel McArthur, gifted me a book by Robin Sharma called *Who Will Cry When You Die?* [6] for my birthday. My initial thoughts on seeing the title were, *"What a strange book to give someone on their birthday!"*

I had recently completed my Reiki training with Isobel and trusted that any book she gifted me would be mind-expanding and for my highest good; I was right. The title can be interpreted in many ways, but at its core, it asks readers to consider what kind of legacy they want to leave behind. The title comes from an ancient Sanskrit expression and means when we are born, we come into this world crying while everyone around us rejoices; when we die, we rejoice a life well lived, yet all around us are crying.

A few years after receiving the book, I attended a two-day program with Robin Sharma[7] called *The Eight Rituals of Visionary Leaders* in Dubai. One of the exercises was to sit in circles of eight to ten people. While we were sitting in silence, we had to write our own eulogy and put it in an envelope with rose petals, whilst listening to the soundtrack from the funeral scene in the movie *Braveheart*[8]. We were then invited to stand in the same circle and share what we wrote by reading it out to the group, or seal the envelope and simply listen to what others had written. To date, this is one of the most powerful exercises I have done to help me make sure I live my life in such a way that everything I wrote in my eulogy is achieved before I pass. It's why, whenever I feel myself going off track, I open the envelope and read it again as a great reminder to get things done.

Here's the first sentence I wrote:

Julie was a woman who made a difference through encouraging everyone she met to live their wildest dreams NOW in the spirit of adventure.

Happy to share the rest when we meet in person and do the same exercise!

Ultimately the *'Who will cry when you die?'* question aims to inspire us to live a life of passion and purpose, by focusing on the things that are true to our values and aspirations.

JOURNAL PROMPT

Time for some deep work! Open your journal and start writing your own eulogy. Take some time to do this without being disturbed.

- Who will be there?
- What will your family, friends and clients say?
- What wild stories will they have to share about you and the legacy you created?
- If you were to die tomorrow, would you consider that you had lived a good life?
- If not, what are you willing to change to make it so?
- Who will cry when you die?
- What would you write in a letter to your loved ones to read after you have passed?

Here's a short note my father wrote before he passed in 2019.

Dear Dorothy and family,
Weep not for me when I am gone. Just think of all the things we have done.
The joy, the sorrow and the grief held us together in our love and belief. But now it's ended, life must go on. Enjoy tomorrow and try to have fun.
Your loving husband,
Reginald

From time to time, I revisit this note and recommit to keep having fun.

"Tears are the summer showers to our soul."
Alfred Austin (1835 – 1913)
English Poet Laureate

COMIC RELIEF

Have you have laughed so much that your eyes started to water? My mum was a champion at shedding tears of laughter, mostly in response to something or someone funny like Tommy Cooper, a British comedian she loved to watch on TV. For Mum, laughter was a natural response. She would often start laughing for no apparent reason. Her laughter was so contagious that everyone around her would crack open with deep belly laughs. The good news is that laughter strengthens your immune system and emotional well-being. It possesses a natural remarkable power to uplift and energise your spirits. It's one of the most therapeutic releases to relieve stress, tension and anxiety, and it's FREE! The truth is, when we laugh or cry, we eventually become more relaxed, strengthen our social connections and are much more able to tackle any challenges we face. Give laughter yoga a go – it's a hoot!

How often do you laugh? Apparently, children laugh hundreds of times a day, as opposed to adults who laugh a mere 15–16 times.[9]

It's clearly time for adults to have more fun, which brings us to a small body of water that invites us to make a splash, be more playful and HAVE FUN!

PUDDLE - PLAYFULNESS

*"Puddle: a small body of water that attracts
other small bodies wearing dry shoes!"*

Anon

Puddles are liquid invitations to play and make a splash. As adults we tend to avoid them, while children run and jump into them with wild abandon. I think avoiding puddles is a sign of getting older which is why you will see me jumping in puddles for the sheer youth-boosting fun of it!

When I was a student at Sheffield Hallam University back in the seventies, I had a pair of bright yellow Wellington boots that I loved wearing on rainy days (I wore them even if it was sunny!). There are lots of rainy days in the UK, so I got plenty of wear out of them. I certainly stood out from the crowd, more so when I jumped into puddles! Interestingly, I found I was much more productive and creative after being playful. REMEMBER TO PLAY!

Neuroscience shows us that there is a relationship between happiness and creativity, suggesting that a positive emotional state can have a beneficial impact on creative thinking. Dopamine, a neurotransmitter associated with pleasure and reward, plays a role in motivation and creative thinking. When we experience positive emotions, it leads to increased dopamine release which may, in turn, enhance creative problem solving and innovation. The 'broaden-and-build' theory of positive emotions proposed by psychologist Dr. Barbara Fredrickson[10] in 2004 suggests that positive emotions broaden our attention and thinking patterns. When people are happy, they tend to think more broadly, consider a wider range of ideas and explore new possibilities – all of which are essential components of creativity.

PUDDLES

Formed by raindrops falling from the sky and dried up by the sun, puddles are a simple symbol of the cycle of life and renewal. They may be small and temporary, yet they have the power to bring a sense of mischievous fun and joy to the heart. Next time you see a puddle, try and look at it through the eyes of a child. It will remind you of the beauty of small things and the importance of having fun. Often the things we try to avoid, such as puddles, can be the very tonic we need.

Years ago, I remember teaching a circuit training class on a lawn area in Dubai and halfway through the session, all the sprinklers came on. It was interesting to see who leapt out of the way and who burst into laughter as they got soaking wet; I was the latter! I have fond memories of water pistol fights with my brother, Paul. As toddlers, it was an empty washing-up liquid bottle that became our watery weapon of choice. As we got older, we had proper water pistols. Even more fun was the garden hose, which is an easy way to ramp up the energy at any garden party! I can recall squeals of joy and raucous laughter. YOU ARE NEVER TOO OLD TO PLAY!

Letting the innocent part of you come out to play is a great way to tap into the energy and joy of our younger years. As a child, everything in my world was alive with the wonders of exploration and sensation. I like to bring this childlike quality to my retreats and expeditions and encourage clients to see all of nature as if for the first time; to operate from what's known as a 'beginner's mind'. When this happens, our sense of awe and wonder is restored; we can begin to appreciate each new day as an adventure.

JOURNAL PROMPT

Time for a puddle break! Take out your journal and answer the following questions:

Is there a part of you that thinks being playful is being childish?

When was the last time you connected to the more youthful parts of yourself?

Do you avoid puddles?

Do you pull your children away from puddles, or are you a wild-hearted parent that jumps in with your kids?

Do you want a partner who lays down his or her jacket and carries you over a puddle?

Or how about one that grabs your hand and jumps into the puddle with you?!

PUDDLE THINKING

Without more rain, puddles become stagnant and eventually evaporate. They don't have the power to move and change without the wind, rain and sun. When we rest on our laurels, operate from a fixed mindset, and expect external forces to guide our growth and transformation, we limit ourselves. The changes need to be internally driven with a growth mindset.

The phrase *'make a splash'* is a common expression that encourages us to attract attention or create an impact with one's actions. I use it as an invitation to clients to:

- Take bold or innovative steps
- Stand out from the crowd
- Grab people's attention
- Take risks
- Develop a unique style that sets them apart
- Get out of their comfort zone
- Strike up conversations with people they don't know
- Try something new/shake things up
- Rediscover their youth

The late Douglas Adams once delivered what he called the 'Parable of the Puddle'[11]. It's an interesting and relevant one to share, so here it is…

"… *imagine a puddle waking up one morning and thinking, 'This is an interesting world I find myself in – an interesting hole I find myself in – fits me rather neatly, doesn't it? In fact, it fits me staggeringly well – must have been made to have me in it!' … as the sun rises in the sky … the puddle gets smaller and smaller, frantically hanging on to the notion that everything's going to be alright, because this world was meant to have him in it; so the moment he disappears catches him rather by surprise. I think this may be something we need to be on the watch out for."*

This parable is very relevant in business, life and relationships.

JOURNAL PROMPT

Take out your journal, take a water break and spend some time answering the questions below.

How can you make a splash in your business?

How can you bring the element of play into your business?

How can you prevent stagnation in your business, life and relationships?

What do puddles represent and symbolise for you?

If a puddle could speak, what would it say to you?

ADVICE FROM A PUDDLE

"Make a splash.
Have some fun.
Play with me.
Jump in!
Accept impermanence and change.
Enjoy me now, I won't be here for long!"
Julie M. Lewis

Let's move on to bigger, permanent puddles – LAKES!

LAKE – REFLECTION

"A lake is a landscape's most beautiful and expressive feature. It is Earth's eye; looking into which the beholder measures the depth of his own nature."
Henry David Thoreau

Every morning after a twenty-minute meditation, I write down three to five things that I would like to bring into my day. I write down whatever comes to mind, and it can change from day to day. For many months, *"Peace of mind"* was at the top of my list. Three simple words, yet I believe they are the foundation of self-mastery. One thing for sure is that a peaceful mind makes better decisions and comes up with better solutions to challenges than a turbulent mind. A peaceful mind is like a sturdy ship equipped to weather any storm that comes its way. The single most valuable thing you can have is a CALM, PEACEFUL MIND. A troubled mind often means chaos.

When I think of peace of mind, I think of a crystal-clear, expansive lake. I take myself there physically or mentally to practice my 'Triple S Factor':

STILLNESS
SILENCE
SOLITUDE

What do I do? Nothing! I simply sit in stillness, silence and solitude until my head clears and new answers to my questions arise. When you combine this practice with reaching out to trusted friends, colleagues, coaches or mentors for alternative perspectives, you have a winning combination.

The calm surface of a lake represents peace and stillness. It's an invitation to reflect, slow down and turn our gaze inward. Lakes hold wisdom, untold stories and secrets that can spark greater creativity and inspiration.

"Make your heart like a lake with a still calm surface
and great depths of kindness."
Lao Tzu

Some of the words that spring to mind when I think of a lake are:

- Serenity
- Tranquillity
- Mystery
- Depth
- Renewal
- Connection

"Lakes are where memories are made, and stories are told."
Anon

In many cultures, lakes are associated with cleansing, renewal, rebirth and purification. There are many legends and myths associated with lakes, the Loch Ness Monster and the Lady of the Lake to name but two.

JOURNAL PROMPT

What legends and myths around lakes are you aware of?

Who told you about them?

What lessons can you take from such legends and myths?

MY FAVOURITE LAKE

In 2015, I took a small group of clients to Tibet to hike around Mount Kailash, a sacred mountain referred to as the "navel of the universe". After the trek, we took a long drive to Lake Manasarovar, located at 4,950m above sea level. The lake covers around 320 square kilometres and is fed by several glacial streams. Its crystal-clear waters surrounded by snow-capped peaks make it a breathtaking sight and experience for those lucky and fit enough to get there!

It's considered one of the most sacred lakes in Hinduism, Buddhism and Jainism. According to Hindu mythology, Lake Manasarovar was created in the mind of Lord Brahma, the creator of the universe. Its name "Mana Sarovar" is derived from Sanskrit words meaning "mind" and "lake". It is believed to be the physical manifestation of the divine lake that existed in Lord Brahma's mind. In Buddhism, the lake is associated with Mount Kailash, the dwelling place of the Buddha of compassion. Buddhists believe that completing a "kora" (walking around the mountain) of Mount Kailash, followed by a dip in the holy waters of Lake Manasarovar, will cleanse the sins of a lifetime and bring spiritual liberation.

We managed to arrive in time for the magic hour of sunset when the lake became one huge reflective mirror. Sitting quietly beside the lake, we could all feel its special energy flowing to and through us. We walked close enough to the lake to see our own reflection and the rocks lying below. There's something very special about seeing your reflection in a lake. I remember thinking of Carl Jung's quote[12].

"Your visions will become clear only when you can look into your own heart.... Who looks outside, dreams; who looks inside, awakes."

Sitting beside the lake, I looked deep within my own heart and felt the raw, honest beauty of the lake infuse every cell of my body. I made a pact to carry that energy for as long as I live, knowing that whenever I need to tap into it, I can close my eyes, visualise myself by the lake and access this special energy all over again.

JOURNAL PROMPT

Take out your journal and write down a few notes about your experience of spending time in, on or around lakes.

- Where were you? Who were you with?
- What words do you think of when you think of a lake?
- How can you be more like a lake?
- What clarity and insights have you experienced sitting by a lake?
- If a lake could speak, what would it say to you?

This week, see if you can sit by a lake, switch off your phone and breathe deeply and slowly for at least ten minutes, and practice the 'Triple S Factor' of Stillness, Silence and Solitude. Take this as a natural opportunity to look within to gain clarity and insight as you retreat from the noise and distractions of the outer world. You will then access what I call your inner GPS, aka your INTUITION.

If you can't get to a lake, clear your mind of turbulence by imagining and visualising it being a still, deep, crystal-clear lake, allowing you to escape the pressures of life. Get into the habit of taking ten minutes for yourself, ideally in the morning when you are relaxed and fresh after a good night's sleep. Close your eyes, centre yourself, visualise bathing in your inner lake of wisdom and ask for guidance for the day ahead. This is a great opportunity to be led by the depth and wisdom in your heart.

"Within you, there is a stillness and a sanctuary
to which you can retreat at any time."
Hermann Hesse

JOURNAL PROMPT

- When you look at yourself in the lake, what do you see?
- Do you like what you see?
- Are you seeing a true reflection of your thoughts, feelings and beliefs as they are now?
- Are these thoughts supporting you or holding you back?
- Write down your answers. Are there any surprises?

"Your inner stillness and reflection bring enlightenment …
you see situations in a strange new light."
The *I Ching*, Ancient Chinese divination text

The more silent and still you can become, the more clearly and directly your intuition will speak to you. Learn to rest in the stillness of the lake within you and savour the silence that brings you more clarity.

"The still waters of a lake reflect the beauty all around it.
When the mind is still, the beauty of the self is reflected within."
B.K.S Iyengar (1918 – 2014),
Indian author and founder of Iyengar Yoga

The image of a calm, clear lake represents the state of inner tranquillity and emotional balance, while a turbulent, muddy lake symbolises a state of confusion and emotional upheaval. When your mind is still, everything is clear; when your mind is turbulent, nothing is clear! We know water can be calm, gentle and supportive, but it can also be fierce, disruptive and unsettling. Whatever you are going and growing through, I guarantee that taking time out to reflect will pay dividends.

"Let the waters settle and you will see the moon and the
stars mirrored in your own being."
Rumi

SOUL QUEST

At the beginning of 2023, I decided to take a different approach to my personal development and signed up for a MYSTERYM program with Mary-Rita McGuire[13] whom I had met at a friend's birthday party. I was intrigued by Mary-Rita's studies and expertise in transpersonal psychology, performing arts, creativity and the journey path transformation process.

In the first session, I decided that the name of my quest for the nine weeks ahead would be **Soul Quest**. For me, a soul quest is a journey of self-discovery and spiritual growth with a focus on connecting with one's deepest sense of purpose. It's an opportunity to define where you are now, where you would like to be and exploring different routes to get there.

When you are in the middle of a transition from the old to the new, as I was, it's a great way to play between worlds before taking strides into the new world you wish to create. For me, it was as if I were standing in the middle of a bridge with one foot in the old world and the other in the new world to be created. Through a series of guided meditations, visualisations, art, role-playing and creative practices, I gained a clearer picture of the new ways I wanted to bring people together.

The concept of a soul quest is rooted in many ancient spiritual traditions, including Shamanism, Buddhism and Hinduism. It often entails going on a physical journey to connect more deeply with the natural world, spending periods of time alone, using silent energy practices such as meditation, prayer and plant medicine. For me, it was a weekly walk to Mary-Rita's home followed by spending time on a bridge contemplating the steps I would need to take to fully cross it into the next chapter of offerings.

REFLECTION IS A SUPERPOWER

In 1933, the philosopher and educator John Dewy wrote, *"We do not learn from experience, we learn from reflecting on experience."*[14]

Harvard Business School had conducted numerous studies that emphasise the benefits of reflection in leadership and personal growth. One prominent figure associated with Harvard Business School and the concept of reflection is the late Chris Argyris, a renowned organisational theorist. His 1974 paper on 'double-loop learning' and 'reflection in action'[15] has been influential in the field of organisational learning and leadership development. His ideas emphasise the importance of individuals and organisations reflecting on their actions and questioning underlying assumptions in order to improve and adapt.

I make it a ritual to reflect on my day before I sleep, and ask myself a selection of simple reflective questions:

- What did I learn today?
- Who or what brought me joy today?
- Whom did I support and who supported me today?
- What went well today?
- What could I do differently tomorrow?
- What was my primary focus today? Did it align with my values?
- How did I take care of myself today?
- What new solutions to my challenges can I consider?

When I lead expeditions or retreats, we have lively discussions in the evening around a meal to recount the day's experience. I open the conversation by asking the group to relate to their senses and share what they saw, heard, tasted, touched or felt along the journey. It's interesting to listen to the answers because we all walked, cycled or kayaked the same route, yet we all experienced something different through our senses. What was significant for one person might have been totally missed by another. It certainly makes people more present and attentive the next day!

Have fun coming up with your own reflective questions. Ask your kids what they learnt at school today. Ask your partner how their day went and truly listen to what they had to say. Do this at work at the end of each day instead of waiting for a weekly or monthly review. Ten to fifteen minutes before everyone leaves for the day creates much stronger engagement and primes everyone for a better tomorrow.

When you take the time to do this consistently, you will see a huge difference in your creativity, decision-making, relationships, self-awareness and gratitude levels.

I find that the best time for personal reflection is at the end of the day before sleep, as it allows more cognitive and emotional processing. Find a time that works best for you. It could be over lunch, during dinner or when you are taking a walk. It can also be useful to do this during the day when you experience a situation or conversation where you feel you need to step back and reflect before you answer or act. Some people call it a "cooling off" period, others suggest "sleeping on it." Whatever you like to call it, reflection is a fantastic practice to wire into your day.

JOURNAL PROMPT

Reach for your *Uncharted Waters* journal and a pen. Make notes on this chapter based on the three pointers below:

 Waves of Wisdom: three ideas – 'ah ha' moments – you had as a result of reading this chapter.

 Neptune's Trident: three actions you can take from reading this chapter.

 Positive ripples: find three people you can talk to about this chapter to create positive ripples.

In the next chapter, we will explore another 'Triple S Factor' – Steam, Streams and Springs!

WATER
IS
ENERGY

CHAPTER FIVE

STEAM, STREAMS, SPRINGS
RELEASE - FLOW - DETERMINATION

"You are water, I am water. We are all water in different containers, that's why it's so easy to meet; someday we'll evaporate together."

Yoko Ono

Japanese multimedia artist, singer and peace activist

WHERE DO YOU GO AND what do you do when you need to let off steam?

Who or what triggers stress and the need for you to let off steam?

Who is your go-to person when you need to talk something through or vent?

'Letting off steam' is a common metaphor for releasing built-up stress or frustration. It's a great way to discharge emotional and mental pressure, and has a positive effect on our overall well-being. While it's beneficial, it's also important to find healthy and constructive ways to do so. Yelling and screaming works for some people but lashing out at others often ends in remorse and it's not great being on the receiving end either! Even the most composed of us need a release at some point.

The best way to let off steam for me is physical activity. It's usually a long beach walk, a swim, the gym, a good shake out, a cold shower or roaring like a lion! I make sure to do my lion roar when there's no one around.

Moving your body moves your mind and gets the feel-good hormones flying around again. More passive ways are journaling, talking things through with a good listener, breathwork, meditation, creative outlets or actually going into a steam room to sweat it all out!

Everyone has different preferences and it's a good idea to find out what works best for you. As a self-regulation strategy, I suggest having a go-to list of activities to choose from when you need to release pent-up stress.

ATTENTION RESTORATION

I am known for my outgoing adventurous spirit. It's one of the ways I release my inner fire. Being active in the great outdoors is like food and oxygen for me. It's one of the best ways to tap into what I call *'big picture thinking'* and what is referred to as 'attention restoration' as a way of balancing out the time spent indoors looking at screens, which is known as 'directed attention'. Rachel and Stephen Kaplan are environmental psychologists known for their groundbreaking work on Attention Restoration Theory, (ART). In their 1989 study, 'The Experience of Nature,'[1] they proposed that exposure to nature or natural environments can help restore mental fatigue and improve directed attention.

UNDER PRESSURE

Building blueprints for joy, health and freedom means being mindfully self-aware; it means knowing and understanding your triggers so that you can offset them and self-regulate. Steam is created when water reaches its boiling point, representing the build-up of stress and tension in our lives. It's important to recognise and manage this pressure. Steam serves as a release valve for pressure, allowing excess energy to escape, so similarly we need to find release valves of our own. Steam represents the need for balance; too much can be explosive, too little can lead to stagnation. The ability to express all our emotions in a constructive manner prevents emotional overload. Expressing your needs, setting healthy boundaries and being open about your expectations all help to resolve any potential conflicts.

Steam is also a symbol of transformation and change. It's a reminder that even the most solid and stable of all things can change given the right conditions. It's also a symbol of possibility and shape-shifting. Steam's ability to shape-shift from water to vapour and back again reminds us that we too can transform ourselves and adapt swiftly to the environment we find or place ourselves in. Steam can also be comforting! Think of the steam rising from a hot drink on a cold day, relaxing in a steam bath, or the fun of doodling on steamy windows! Steam power was a driving force behind the Industrial Revolution, enabling the mechanisation of various industries, revolutionising transportation and increasing the overall productivity of society. This period of industrialisation had far-reaching effects on economies, societies and technologies, and laid the foundation for modern industrialised nations today.

The benefits of letting off steam are numerous. Here are my top five!

- ⬥ Stress reduction
- ⬥ Improved mental health

- Enhanced self-awareness
- Increased productivity
- Strengthened relationships

IDEAS FOR LETTING OFF STEAM WITH WATER

1. **Take a warm bath.** Taking a warm bath is a great way to relieve stress. Dim the lights, light a candle, add bath salts or essential oils, play some instrumental music, and let the warm water relax your muscles and calm your mind.

2. **Go for a swim.** Swimming is one of my favourite ways to relieve stress as it flips me from cortisol to endorphin release. I switch into a calming meditative state, my mind clears, and I become very present in the now. Just the water, my breath and my body moving through the water.

3. **Listen to the sound of water.** I have a small 'sounds of nature' box which plays different sounds of water. It's possible to play them all at once or individually. It's a great on-the-spot alternative if you can't get to a body of water. There are several apps and websites offering the sound of waterfalls, rivers, rain or the ocean.

4. **Floating meditation.** I take my mask and snorkel to the beach or pool and float face downwards focusing on my breath. It's a great way to let go and experience the feeling of weightlessness, of being supported by the water. Combine it with intentional breathing – as you exhale, release all your worries, and as you inhale, welcome in what you wish to experience such as peace, calm, focus and joy.

5. **Take a cold shower or ice bath.** Time to channel your inner Wim Hof! I find taking a cold shower or an

ice bath is a fast and easy way to reduce stress, boost my circulation and feel more alert. I take cold showers across the day whenever I feel my energy dipping or I literally need to cool down (which, living in the Middle East, is quite often!). It's the exact opposite of taking a hot bath, so choose which one works best for you.

6. **Take a walk near water.** Walking near water is a natural stress buster. The negative ions have a positive impact on your mood. It's another one of my favourites with top of the list being a barefoot walk on the beach for as long as I need to switch from stressed to blessed.

7. **Have a good cry, water the garden, jump in puddles or have a colonic!**

8. **Put the kettle on and make a pot of tea!** Sipping and savouring tea is good for the soul.

9. **Try a float tank (also called an isolation tank or sensory deprivation tank).** This is essentially the perfect bath tub. They vary in size and the door never locks or latches so air is allowed to freely flow in and out. The water within is saturated with 1,000 pounds of Epsom salt to create a solution more buoyant than the Dead Sea. You float on your back, half in and half out of the water. The tank is soundproof and when you turn off the light, it is completely dark. No gravity, no touch, no sound – pure nothing!

10. **Try Watsu.** Watsu is a form of aquatic bodywork and therapy that combines elements of water massage and stretching. It was developed in the early 1980s by Harold Dull[2], a California-based practitioner, to include the principles of Zen Shiatsu with the therapeutic properties of warm water.

STREAM - FLOW

I love wandering around bookshops. If we ever go shopping together and you can't find me, then head straight to the nearest bookstore! I normally head for the personal development, travel, business and spiritual development sections and randomly pick up titles that I am drawn to. Flipping through the pages of a book is a great opportunity to enter a different stream of consciousness. To dive into the head of the author and get lost in new streams of thoughts, ideas and concepts.

Stream of consciousness is a narrative technique in literature that aims to capture the continuous flow of a character's thoughts and perceptions as they occur in real-time. It provides readers with insight into the inner workings of a character's mind, often revealing their innermost thoughts, emotions, memories and associations without a structured or linear narrative. Pioneered by authors like James Joyce and Virginia Woolf, stream of consciousness writing immerses readers in the subjective experiences of characters, offering a unique and often intimate perspective on the human psyche. This approach invites readers to explore the complexity of thought and consciousness, emphasising the richness and unpredictability of our inner mental landscapes.

Whenever I see a stream, it reminds me of the importance of vital energy flow and the power of perseverance in achieving our goals. Water is known for seeking its own level, form and balance. As humans, we do well to seek the same within ourselves. When we feel balanced, our energy flows more smoothly. When we feel out of balance and off form, our energy can stagnate or, worse still, become blocked and manifest as physical, mental or emotional dis-ease.

The concept of tapping into a stream of universal energy often relates to spiritual or metaphysical beliefs and practices. One of my favourite ways to tap into the energy source beyond the physical world is through meditation. Other ways include yoga, mindfulness, Reiki and energy healing practices, nature, and prayer. I am a big fan of Kelly Howell[3]. Kelly is a well-known figure in the field of guided meditation and brainwave entrainment. She has created a variety of meditation tracks and programs designed to help individuals enter altered states of consciousness, achieve relaxation and experience personal growth. I enjoy listening to Kelly's The Secret Universal Mind Meditation, as it focuses on aligning your consciousness with the universal mind to promote personal growth, creativity and a deeper sense of connection with the universe.

Scan the QR code to hear the meditation for yourself.

Water is also a great way to help you enter a different stream of consciousness. Floatation tanks, also known as sensory deprivations tanks, are filled with saltwater at body temperature, allowing you to float effortlessly. The combination of sensory deprivation, buoyancy and a quiet environment promotes deep relaxation and altered states of consciousness. I haven't tried this yet; however, when I float in the sea, I feel as if I have been taken through a portal into an altered state of connection and consciousness. The sound of flowing water or waves lapping the shore can help you enter a deeper state of awareness and presence. The sound of a running stream can induce trance-like states like listening to Tibetan singing bowl, gongs or crystals.

The Map of Consciousness[4] by David Hawkins is a conceptual framework that categorises different levels of human consciousness based on their vibrational frequency or emotional and spiritual quality. It ranges from lower levels associated with negative emotions and limiting beliefs (e.g., shame, guilt and fear) to higher levels characterised by positive emotions and expanded awareness (e.g., love, joy and peace). The map suggests that as individuals raise their level of consciousness, they experience greater well-being, clarity and spiritual growth, while lower levels are associated with more negative and limited states of mind. It's a tool for understanding and measuring one's state of awareness and personal growth. There is a strong connection between an individual's level of consciousness and their ability to experience flow. Individuals who operate at higher levels of consciousness – such as courage, acceptance and beyond – are far more likely to enter states of flow. This is because higher states of consciousness are associated with increased clarity and creativity, and a sense of interconnectedness and flow is considered a higher state of consciousness. When we are in flow, we lose track of time. I have experienced this when swimming, hiking, writing and, more generally, doing things that bring me joy!

Scan the QR code to view the Map of Consciousness.

Earlier I talked about water as the elixir of life and its essential role in all ecosystems. When I think of streams, I think of the veins in our bodies connecting to arteries (rivers) and all our major organs (our body/the planet). Streams remind me of the interconnectedness of all living beings, that we are all part of a larger whole, and our energy and actions impact everything and everyone around us. As every stream has its own flow, each of us needs to find our own rhythm and flow. This means knowing what your values are and consciously living them, understanding your strengths, having a clear vision, and adopting daily healthy lifestyle habits that resonate with and support your flow. By being mindfully self-aware, making self-care a priority and living your values, you are much more likely to experience a healthy flow of energy.

If a stream could speak, what would it say to you?

When you are in flow, you can SPRING into action which leads us onto one of the smallest yet most resilient bodies of water: a SPRING.

SPRING - DETERMINATION

What words do you think of when you think of a spring?

The first words I think of are **determination, resilience, focus** and **inner resources**. Springs are a source of fresh water that continually emerges from the earth. They overcome rocks and terrain, and harness the power of underground water sources to push through and provide nourishment to the surrounding vegetation. Likewise, in our lives, we need to be determined and persevere in the face of obstacles, able to tap into our wellspring of inner resources, to push through to nurture our potential and support our growth. As springs maintain a natural balance of inflow and outflow to ensure a continuous and sustainable water supply, we need to find a balance between self-care and forging ahead with our goals. As springs adapt their flow to changing seasons and weather conditions, we too need to be open to change to new circumstances and new experiences. As springs have a connection to underground water sources, we too need to stay connected to our inner core of resources as we persevere on our journey of self-improvement.

A spring of water keeps flowing consistently regardless of the external conditions or obstacles. They often emerge from a rocky or dry terrain symbolising that we, as individuals, can overcome challenges and obstacles in our paths. Springs don't run dry easily, emphasising the importance of staying committed to your goals. Springs flow in a specific direction following a natural path. This aligns with the concept of focus and the importance of channelling one's efforts towards a specific goal or purpose.

If a spring could speak, what would it say to you?

What does it feel like to be a spring? It means having a resilient spirit, unwavering determination, and the ability to channel your energy and efforts toward your goals despite challenges. It's about maintaining a positive and forward-focused mindset, bouncing forward and stronger from setbacks, and experiencing the satisfaction of achieving what you set out to do. BE A SPRING.

FOUNTAIN OF YOUTH

The Fountain of Youth is a legendary spring that is believed to have rejuvenating properties. According to the legend, anyone who drinks from the fountain will be granted eternal youth and beauty. The Fountain of Youth concept is still present in various cultures. It is commonly associated with the Spanish explorer Juan Ponce de León, who searched for the fountain in Florida in the early sixteenth century. There is no significant evidence to support the theory, yet there are plenty of claims for various products that promise to slow down the effects of ageing and offer miracle beauty solutions. When you find one, please let me know...!

JOURNAL PROMPT

Reach for your *Uncharted Waters* journal and a pen.
Make notes on this chapter based on the three pointers
below:

 Waves of Wisdom: three ideas – 'ah ha'
moments – you had as a result of reading
this chapter.

 Neptune's Trident: three actions you
can take from reading this chapter.

 Positive ripples: find three people you
can talk to about this chapter to create
positive ripples.

In the next chapter, we explore the flow and power of
rivers, the sea and the ocean.

WATER
IN
FLOW

Chapter Six

River, Sea, Ocean
Resilience - Support - Emotions

"Beautiful, mysterious, wild and free."
Julie M. Lewis

FROM FRAZZLED TO FLOW

IN AN 'ALWAYS ON' ever-changing world, it's easy to burn out. Our minds and bodies are not made to operate in *'fight, flight or freeze mode'* for long periods of time. Unless we take time to balance high-intensity periods with quality recovery time, it's easy to become frazzled.

When we keep pushing against the current and ignore our need to rest and rejuvenate, our central nervous system becomes frazzled, our immune system is compromised and our ability to think clearly is impacted.

My river of resilience was dangerously low after two years of being the primary caregiver and patient advocate for Calin. Brain surgery, radiotherapy, immunotherapy, and two years of being in and out of ICU took a toll on both of us. I quickly learnt that it is super important to triple your self-care during challenging times. When we don't, the body eventually stops us in our tracks.

This happened to me in December 2019. I was on a long flight to Denver to join Calin and the family for a white Christmas and New Year in Steamboat Springs, Colorado. The day after I arrived in Steamboat, I went to the local sports club, worked out in the gym, then had a quick swim, followed by a dip in the hot springs. This is a usual post-flight routine to help me recalibrate. Twenty-four hours later, I was bedridden with a high fever, banging headache and achy body. What happened? I figured the last two years had finally caught up with me and my body simply shut down. Whatever it was, it was a clear message telling me to stop everything and REST.

I was in bed for six days while everyone else was partying! I had to let go and simply surrender, which, as an Aries, is not my style. I spent all of Christmas, New Year's Eve and New Year's Day in bed. Finally, on 2nd January 2020, I felt well enough to get out of bed and be social again. I made a promise to myself from that day on that I would practice what I preach and balance periods of intensity with quality recovery time (QRT)!

"To stay present in everyday life, it helps to be deeply rooted in yourself; otherwise, the mind, which has incredible momentum, will drag you along like a wild river."
Eckhart Tolle, German-born spiritual teacher and author

RIVERS

Some of the most symbolic meanings associated with rivers are those of:

- Life
- Vitality
- Journeys
- Purification

- ◆ Transition
- ◆ Change
- ◆ Connection
- ◆ Unity
- ◆ Power
- ◆ Mystery
- ◆ Flow
- ◆ Resilience

As we learned in the previous chapter, the expression *"go with the flow"* is a great metaphor for life and is the perfect metaphor for navigating a river. When we go with the flow, we work with the current of the river rather than pushing against it. To truly go with the flow requires awareness, presence and intuitive resilience. Going with the flow doesn't mean we toss our oars into the water and hope for the best; it means noticing the play of energy all around us. It means being flexible in our approach and being open to multiple ways of getting to where we want to be.

> *"Do a good deed and throw it in the river,*
> *one day it will come back to you in the desert."*
>
> Rumi

Most of us are afraid of going with the flow because we don't trust that we will get where we want to go. The *'my way or the highway'* approach can cause us to cling to plans that aren't working, stick to routes that are obstructed and obsess over relationships that are no longer fulfilling.

Mental, emotional, spiritual and physical tension comes from unmet expectations and from holding on to old patterns, habits and behaviours. When we insist on staying in our comfort zone, we literally stunt our own growth and potential. As a river adapts to its environment, we also need to adapt to changing circumstances and continue moving forward. During times of great change, it can feel like there is a strong rapid river gushing through all areas of our lives. When we surrender to this flowing energy, we can move with it and become part of it, like a small twig that floats on the surface of the water. If we cling to the shores of old patterns, old beliefs, behaviours and emotions, eventually we start to feel frazzled and overwhelmed. The best way to deal with this vast flowing energy is to trust the flow and embrace the changes it brings.

If a river could speak, what would it say to you?

Sometimes the river of life takes us to places we don't want to or didn't expect to go. When this happens, my advice is to let go or be dragged. We use a lot of energy holding on. Loosen your grip on the riverbanks of your life and relinquish the need for control. When you have the courage to do this, you open yourself up to opportunities beyond your current imagination.

The quote *"You cannot step into the same river twice"* is often attributed to the ancient Greek philosopher Heraclitus. This statement embodies the philosophical idea that everything in the world is constantly changing and in a state of flux. Each moment in life is unique and can never be replicated the same way. The quote encourages us to accept change instead of holding onto the past or resist the future.

JOURNAL PROMPT

Take out your *Uncharted Waters* journal and answer the questions below. When you look at your life or business over the last five years, try and identify periods when:

- You experienced flow
- You felt drained
- You felt stagnant
- You were trying to control the uncontrollable
- You felt totally out of your depth
- You experienced resistance

How did you flip out of being drained, stagnant or out of your depth?

Have you ever been white-water rafting? My first experience of white-water rafting was in Sri Lanka on the Kelani River, Kitulgala with a group of my clients. The location is steeped in history as it's where *The Bridge on the River Kwai*[1] was filmed, making it quite a nostalgic experience. We had fun kitting up in full wetsuits, booties and helmets ready for a wet and wild ride. There was a huge sense of excitement and anticipation at the start – none of us had rafted before. However, we had sea-kayaked and were all very comfortable in water so figured we would soon get used to the surge of adrenaline as we hit the first set of rapids.

The physical sensation of the raft bouncing and splashing through the water was exhilarating! I am sure there was a little fear mixed in with the excitement. I had booked the best guides and equipment so felt pretty sure we would make it down the river and have fun in the process! White-water rafting is a great confidence building activity. Navigating difficult sections of the river gives you a strong sense of accomplishment; the laughter and shared experience on the raft is also pure joy and fun. The opportunity to connect so closely with nature is so powerful. To become one with the river, you experience a sense of awe and wonder at the force of nature and the importance of respecting and preserving it. Lasting memories were made and because I enjoyed the experience so much, it was added into trips to Nepal, South America and Montenegro.

If you have tried white-water rafting, were you able to relax and go with the flow? Or did you find yourself feeling tense and wanting to control your way through the water, regardless of what instructions you were given, or what other team members were doing?

INTUITIVE RESILIENCE

By tapping into our intuitive resilience, we can harness our power and navigate the challenges and obstacles we face in life with much more ease. As a river flows without effort, intuition can help us move through life with greater ease. Intuition is our innate ability to understand or know something instinctively without the need for conscious reasoning. It means getting out of our **thinking** head into our *feeling* heart and **knowing** gut. It's often described as an inner knowing or sense of deep insight. It's a superpower when it comes to making decisions, solving problems and sensing the underlying currents of a situation. Think of a river weaving around rocks, responding to what's below and ahead; this is intuitive resilience in action.

Having trained and led teams of paddlers on dragon boats, snake boats and long boats around the globe, I can say hand on heart that a combination of specific training, discipline and intuitive resilience goes a long way when developing winning teams. The ability to read the river, work with the currents and know exactly when to shift gears from the start, middle and towards the finishing line of the race is a superpower. Paddling competitively on boats give you a huge boost of connection and joy. Paddling with a team creates a unique sense of unity and shared purpose, and fosters a deep bond between everyone on the boat. Racing is physically demanding. The burn you feel in your arms, shoulders and core is both exhausting and invigorating. It takes a lot of concentration and focus to maintain smooth, synchronised powerful strokes together. Each team members contribution is essential for success. It only takes one or two paddlers being out of sync to impact the boat.

Being on water with a thin layer of boat separating you from the water offers a strong connection to the water. You can literally feel the water's ebb and flow around the boat and beneath you. You become one with the water and it's an amazing feeling.

FEAR

If you find that fear of change is keeping you in the same river, I think you will enjoy this analogy from Khalil Gibran...

"It is said that before entering the sea, a river trembles with fear.
She looks back at the path she has travelled, from the peaks of the mountains,
the long winding road crossing forests and villages.
And in front of her, she sees an ocean so vast, that to enter
there seems nothing more than to disappear forever.
But there is no way back. The river cannot go back.
Nobody can go back. To go back is impossible in existence.
The river needs to take the risk of entering the ocean,
because only then will fear disappear,
because that's where the river will know
it's not about disappearing into the ocean,
but of becoming the ocean."

This analogy reminds me of the conversation I had with a fabulous friend, Natalie Hore. We were chatting about our love and connection to water, and she recalled her first experience of learning how to swim and being thrown in the water by her dad at around the age of three. Her dad was always there to scoop her up. However, she said, *"It was a bit of a shock to my system at the time."* She recalled that she was never encouraged to go to the beach. Time was often short as both parents were busy with work. It was only at the age of 28 when her boyfriend Shannon (now her husband) gave her a mask, snorkel and fins and introduced her to a whole new world beneath the waves.

"I remember vividly how much I loved it;
I was just flabbergasted that this underwater world existed."

I think many of us can relate to this as we progress from being on the water to snorkelling or diving below it. When I got my first mask and snorkel as a child, I spent hours in the water looking for treasures and dreamed of being a mermaid so that I could swim down deeper, without having to wear a mask or snorkel!

Over a period of time, Natalie fell in love with scuba diving and SHARKS! *"Although there was a fear of the ocean, there was also a love of it,"* she says. *"When I see all the amazing sea creatures, especially sharks, I have no fear. Once when I was sitting on my knees on the ocean bed, a tiger shark came towards me. She wasn't coming with any aggression; she was gentle and curious. I couldn't believe she choose to spend this moment with me. She went over my shoulder on my left side, and I remember moving my head so her tail wouldn't hit me. I felt the water being swept across my face from the movement of her tail; it was a goosebump moment."*

As Susan Jeffers famously says, *"Feel the fear and do it anyway!"*

I asked Natalie what water would say to her if it could speak, and her instant answer was *"JUMP IN!"*

A SEA OF SUPPORT

*"When I sit here by the sea and listen to the sound of the waves,
I feel free from all obligations and people of this world."*

Henry David Thoreau

SUTTON-ON-SEA

As a child, I was fortunate to spend most summers on the east
coast of England with my parents and siblings. We had a mobile
home in Sutton-on-Sea on the Lincolnshire coast. We spent hours
at the beach, building sandcastles, swimming and collecting shells.
We loved running up and down the beach, hurdling over the
breakwaters, flying kites, enjoying donkey rides, ice cream and
picnics until sunset. Not an iPhone in sight of course in those days!
We made these trips to the coast every Easter and summer. In the
summer, we would stay for six weeks. Dad would drive us over
at the beginning of our summer holidays, have a full week with
us all, then head back to work. Thereafter he would join us on
Friday evenings and stay until late on Sunday afternoons. During
the week, Mum had four of us to keep an eye on. I often wondered
how she managed this; she obviously had a BLUE MIND and
plenty of intuitive resilience! I also know she had support from
other women and families on the caravan site which leads in
beautifully to the concept of a 'sea of support.'

A Sea of Support symbolises an ecosystem of individuals,
resources and relationships that help us in times of need. It
reminds us that we are not alone on our journey and have diverse
support systems to call on: family, friends, mentors, colleagues,
communities and online groups, to name a few. Navigating a
sea of support means actively seeking out and tapping into these
networks when facing challenges, setbacks or during times of
transition. As the sea provides stability, buoyancy and a sense of

security, we can reach out to others to help us find this through human connection.

The marine ecosystem is a complex web of life where countless species of plants and animals coexist and interact in a delicate balance, all while contributing to the health and vitality of the ocean itself. From the smallest plankton to the mightiest predators, every organism plays a crucial role in maintaining the harmony of this underwater world. Phytoplankton, for instance, serve as the foundation of the marine food chain, providing sustenance for zooplankton, which in turn become food for small fish. These smaller fish are essential prey for larger fish, marine mammals and seabirds. The intricate relationships extend further, as coral reefs offer shelter and breeding grounds for numerous species, and kelp forests provide critical habitats. Ultimately, the synergy within the marine ecosystem not only ensures the survival of countless marine species, but also contributes to the ocean's overall health by regulating nutrient cycling, carbon absorption and oxygen production, making it a vital and interconnected system.

This supportive ecosystem can also be found in the forests whereby trees support each other through a network of interconnected roots sharing water and nutrients. Communicating as one ecosystem is a fascinating phenomenon known as 'forest cohesion' or 'tree communication'. Trees in a forest are not isolated individuals. They are part of a larger community – a world wide web! In times of drought or nutrient scarcity, trees with access to more resources can transfer water, nutrients and even carbon to their neighbours in need. This support helps maintain the overall health of the forest and prevents weaker trees from dying off to ensure the ecosystem's resilience and vitality. This collaborative behaviour among trees ensures that no single tree dominates at the expense of others.

VITAMIN SEA

During Calin's cancer treatments, I had to be super resourceful and channel my energy wisely. It would have been very easy to succumb to what scientists call 'co-suffering', a phenomenon whereby 'mirror neurons' absorb the pain and suffering of others.

What could I do to help prevent burning out from the sheer intensity of being in co-suffering and survival mode for extended periods of time?

The answer was found in salty water, the SEA!

I found solace and support in the sea with daily afternoon swims before returning to the hospital. During this time, we lived on a beach development with full access to an open stretch of sea. I would drive home from the hospital, strip off, jump in the shower, wash away the hospital energy, slip into my swimwear, grab my bag and head to the beach. When the sea was rough, I loved the waves crashing into my body, knocking me off my feet and carrying me towards the shoreline. Other times, it was as calm as a lake, and I would swim freestyle for a good hour. Other times, I found myself treading water…

TREADING WATER

During Calin's medical journey, the concept of treading water took on more meaning for me in that I felt that's exactly what we were doing. In between medical appointments, tests, scans, insurance claims and the numerous transfers between ICU and regular wards, we seemed to be in a holding pattern while waiting for better solutions to open up. There were days when little or no progress was made and all we could do was stay afloat, keep our heads above the water and trust that things would shift so we could move on with our plans.

HEALTH BENEFITS

Spending time in or by the sea is a relaxing and restorative sensory experience. It lifts and shifts us from the heaviness of all our cares and concerns. The mere sight of the sea transports us to a whole new world where we can tune in to the sights and sounds of the waves. I love feeling the sand between my toes and letting the water warm or cool my feet. On a biological level, this audio-visual stimulus incites our parasympathetic nervous system. This system, often known as 'rest and digest', conserves energy and facilitates recovery and functions in opposition to the sympathetic nervous system of flight, flight or freeze. It is why you will find me at the beach every day for barefoot walks, meditation and swims as part of my daily grounding and centring rituals.

Salty air is good for you. It helps clear out the lungs and reduces the need for antibiotics. Next time you are by the sea, notice how much easier it is to breathe there compared to the city. Have you also noticed how much better you sleep after time at the beach? Water, sunlight, fresh air and movement are a natural formula for a good night's sleep.

Spending time outdoors by the sea also gives you a natural dose of vitamin D which is key in combating depression, strengthening bones and boosting the immune system. Salt water infuses your skin with magnesium which is important for muscle function, blood coagulation and nutrient metabolism. Salt water is naturally antibacterial. Scrapes, cuts and sores heal much faster after spending time in the sea.

Working out in water is great for easing arthritis and muscle pain, as the buoyancy and resistance of the water make a great combination. My favourite water workout is a swim followed by walking in the water at waist height (sea walking!), finishing off with a floating meditation. It's one of the best ways to feel totally free and connected to myself, just me, the water and my breath.

By the Sea by Dr. Deborah Cracknell[2] reinforces the benefits of being by the sea and its impact on our well-being. Through personal anecdotes and scientific research, her book explores how the sea can improve our lives all the way through physical activity, mindfulness, self-care, ocean conservation, appreciation of the beauty of the sea, reducing stress and anxiety, boosting creativity, and getting a good night's sleep. I resonate with her reference of the sea being a source of inspiration and creativity, and often head to the beach with a pen and notepad in hand.

> *"The sea does not reward those who are too anxious, too greedy, or too impatient. One should lie empty, open, choiceless as the beach – waiting for a gift from the sea."*
> Anne Morrow Lindbergh (1906 – 2001),
> American author and aviator

Gift from the Sea by Anne Morrow Lindbergh[3] is one of my favourite books about the sea. It is organised around the theme of shells to symbolise different stages of a woman's life. Anne emphasises the importance of solitude and introspection, and encourages women to embrace their own path in life, rather than trying to conform to societal expectations.

> *"A woman must come of age by herself. She must find her true center alone."*

I appreciate the way she acknowledges the challenges and contradictions that come with balancing personal aspirations and responsibilities to others. I say that because after graduating from university, I turned down a couple of opportunities that would have taken me away from family. As it worked out, one of those opportunities opened up again when I was 27. I decided to take it and started my first post in the Middle East.

I love the way Anne weaves in the themes of nature, spirituality and creativity, change, loss, and the importance of communication, trust and mutual respect in relationships. Taking weekends away and factoring in at least one personal retreat away from everything and everyone is a must for me. I need 'me time' every day. I highly recommend taking yourself off for an overnighter at a local hotel or guest house to simply 'be and do' what you want to do.

"Too often, I've used up precious time preparing for experiences rather than just having them."

Joan Anderson, American author and journalist

Another of my favourite books is *A Year by the Sea*, a fabulous memoir by Joan Anderson[4] written in 1999, that has also been adapted into a feature film. The book chronicles Joan's journey of self-discovery and personal growth as she spends a year living alone in a cottage by the sea after her children have grown up and her marriage has hit a rough patch. I love the way she reflects on her past, present and future whilst learning to appreciate the simple joys of solitude, nature and self-reliance.

I relate to the way she forms deep connections with the people in the small coastal community where she lives, learning valuable lessons about friendship, love and resilience. This is exactly what I experienced when I spent five weeks living in a caravan in Deal during my training for the English Channel swim – more on this later. I like the honesty and relatable portrayal of the challenges and rewards of mid-life transitions she shares, as well as the celebration of the beauty and power of the natural world. I think there is a bit of Joan in all of us; there's a lot of her in me. For example, what I thought would be a temporary move to a seaside studio in Ras Al Khaimah in the northern emirate of the UAE became my 'year by the sea'. It has become more than one year now!

One of my favourite poems relating to becoming stronger because of the experiences we have, is captured beautifully in Bernadette Noll's poem, *I Want to Age Like Sea Glass.*[5]

I love the poem so much that I have included it here for you, with kind permission from Bernadette.

SEA GLASS

"I want to age like sea glass. Smoothed by tides, not broken. I want the currents of life to toss me around, shake me up and leave me feeling washed clean. I want my hard edges to soften as the years pass – made not weak but supple. I want to ride the waves, go with the flow, feel the impact of the surging tides rolling in and out.

When I am thrown against the shore and caught between the rocks and a hard place, I want to rest there until I can find the strength to do what is next. Not stuck – just waiting, pondering, feeling what it feels like to pause. And when I am ready, I will catch a wave and let it carry me along to the next place that I am supposed to be.

I want to be picked up on occasion by an unsuspected soul and carried along – just for the connection, just for the sake of appreciation and wonder. And with each encounter, new possibilities of collaboration are presented, and new ideas are born.

I want to age like sea glass so that when people see the old woman I'll become, they'll embrace all that I am. They'll marvel at my exquisite nature, hold me gently in their hands and be awed by my well-earned patina. Neither flashy nor dull, just a perfect luster. And they'll wonder, if just for a second, what it is exactly I am made of and how I got to this very here and now. And we'll both feel lucky to be in that perfectly right place at that profoundly right time.

I want to age like sea glass. I want to enjoy the journey and let my preciousness be, not in spite of the impacts of life, but because of them."

When I speak, run retreats and expeditions, I often gift a piece of sea glass to participants as a keepsake to remind them of the power of 'becoming polished' as a result of all the experiences they have weathered.

Scan the QR code to learn more about the back story to the sea glass poem.

JOURNAL PROMPT

Take out your journal and note down what **sea glass experiences** you have had in your life. What did you learn about yourself and others from these experiences?

- Knowing what you know now, what would you do differently?
- What emotions arose as you wrote your experiences down?

Take a break before reading any further and reflect on the experiences you have noted in your journal. Ideally, take a break from reading and go for a walk by a river or the sea to anchor in the insights and learnings. If you can't get out for a walk, soak in the bath, take a refreshing shower, or simply visualise yourself by the sea.

OCEAN OF EMOTIONS

> *"She will be the one.*
> *Standing by the ocean*
> *With the sun in her hair*
> *And a smile like a song*
> *Rising from the sea."*
>
> Printed with permission by Mark Anthony[6]

I associate the ocean with freedom, adventure, infinity, change, power, mystery and emotions. Like the ocean, our emotions can be calm, serene and reassuring, or turbulent, unpredictable and overwhelming. Emotions encompass a wide spectrum of feelings from joy, love and happiness, to anger, sadness, fear and everything in between. As the ocean is influenced by the weather, tides and currents, our emotions are influenced by our thoughts, experiences, relationships and external circumstances.

It is estimated that 80% of our oceans are unexplored, unmapped and unobserved. I wonder how much of our personal ocean of emotions is still unexplored, unmapped and unobserved?

> *"You are not a drop in the ocean, you are an entire ocean in a drop."*
>
> Rumi

Emotions are an important aspect of our lives and experiences; they have a major impact on the way we think, act and feel. As we learn to navigate the currents, waves and tides of the ocean, it is also beneficial to learn to navigate the ebb and flow of our emotions in the quest to lead a healthier, more fulfilling life. Emotions can have a significant impact on our overall health and well-being. Constantly feeling anxious leads to elevated levels of cortisol, chronic stress, muscle tension, headaches and sleep disturbances. Negative emotions can have negative impacts on the mind and body. Anger and hostility are linked with an increased risk of heart disease as it can contribute to high blood pressure and inflammation. Positive emotions, such as happiness, can have a protective effect on health by boosting the immune system, lowering stress hormones and improving cardiovascular health.

Like the tides, our emotions come and go; they are literally energy in motion. Our feelings and emotions are sometimes uncomfortable; they are so for a reason. They are calling for our attention. It's impossible to ignore, repress or escape them. Instead, I invite you to acknowledge them, sit with them for a while, then choose which ones you want to stay and which ones you want to let go, as a sure way to lessen the power they have over you.

Scan the QR code to hear the relaxing sounds of the ocean.

"To be affected by strong emotions and vibration is the best energy source. The more emotion you have every day, the more energetic your life will be."
Dr. Masuru Emoto

HIGHEST EMOTIONAL PRIORITIES

What are your highest emotional priorities?

It's a question that was asked during a virtual workshop a few years ago. It was the first time I had heard the word *priority* linked to emotions. When we are aware of our highest emotional priorities, it is so much easier to make decisions. Decisions about how we spend our time, how we spend our money, who we spend our time with, what we talk about and, ultimately, our relationship with ourselves.

Along with our core values, emotional priorities are the key drivers that come into play every time we make decisions. To help me with my own decision-making process, I spent some time exploring my highest emotional priorities and came up with my top five:

- Joy
- Peace
- Freedom
- Growth
- Love

They align well with my core values of:

- Health
- Joy
- Courage
- Freedom
- Growth
- Relationships
- Adventure
- Making a Difference

When I have a decision to make, I ask myself, *"Does this decision align with my values and highest emotional priorities?"* If it does, it's a clear sign to say yes; if not, it's a clear sign to say no. It's as simple as that.

Emotional flexibility and alchemy are the ability to turn your:

- Pain into power
- Fear into love
- Doubt into clarity
- Chaos in to calm
- Sadness into joy
- Disappointment into curiosity
- Desperation into inspiration
- Hopelessness into hopefulness

TOP TEN POSITIVE EMOTIONS

During the lockdown period, I decided to take a few online courses to add to my portfolio of offerings. I chose several short courses on positive psychology led by Dr. Barbara Fredrickson and was reassured to see two of my top emotional priorities in the list of the top ten positive emotions list.

Simply by being more aware of the top ten positive emotions, we can start to build and boost our emotional fitness by focusing on places, activities and people that elicit these emotions. Here they are:

Joy	Inspiration
Gratitude	Awe
Serenity	Love
Amusement	Interest
Pride	Hope

The goal is to make sure you experience at least five of these emotions every day. If this sounds like a tall order, note that even small micro-moments of connection to the people, places and activities that elicit such emotions, compound to form an overall feeling of positivity. A smile, watching the sunrise, chatting with a friend, patting an animal, being in nature, learning something new, a kiss, a hug, exercising, singing, dancing, the smell of coffee... these are all seemingly small things yet when experienced across the day, they make a big difference.

So as not to seem one-sided or completely blind to other emotions, it's time to get real! There are times in our life when we experience what we have labelled as "negative emotions" such as anger, fear, sadness, guilt and shame. They are neither good nor bad, they simply **are**.

Does your anger or someone else's anger make you feel uncomfortable? Were you taught anger isn't nice or not acceptable to express? Maybe you are in a slow boil all the time and don't know how to take the irons from the fire? In my experience, it's best not to fight with emotions. Let them in with love and kindness, let them have their say. Learn to express them, make them your ally and transform them so they empower and energise you. Choose which ones you'd like to let go and the ones you would like to stay.

Emotions are real-time messages and remind us of our humanness. What we do with these negative emotions can be the difference between staying stuck, spiralling further down to depths of despair, or using them as a catalyst for personal transformation. Discussing negative emotions can provide validation and support. When we share our struggles with family or friends, we often find more empathy and understanding from them. This helps us validate our emotions and can lead on to problem-solving and coping strategies.

Sharing negative emotions can release pent-up stress and tension – **name them to tame them!** By discussing negative emotions openly, we broaden and build our resilience. Open discussions about negative emotions helps reduce the stigma surrounding mental health issues and encourages people to seek help when they need it. Honest conversations about emotions deepens connections and intimacy in relationships allowing for a greater understanding of each other's emotional needs.

WAVES OF EMOTION

Like the waves of the ocean, emotions can come in different intensities, frequencies and rhythms. They can be powerful, fluctuating and cause chaos, or bring about calm. Like the waves, our emotions are not static or predictable; they are dynamic and always changing. Our emotions can shift and evolve over time and range from the highs and lows of a relationship, the ups and downs of life, or the rush of adrenaline and excitement when we connect with our purpose or achieve a long-sought goal. We are often afraid to dive into our emotions, choosing instead to skim the surface.

IT'S JUST A FEELING

When you say, *"Oh, it's just a feeling,"* you are more than likely ignoring an important message. Give yourself space to feel, express and integrate the energy of your emotions as they flow through you.

Feel your feelings, name them to tame them and conduct a quick **emotional audit** with yourself.

- ♦ What are you feeling right now?
- ♦ What or who has caused you to feel this way?
- ♦ What is the gift of this feeling?

- Does this feeling empower you or limit you?
- What would you like to feel instead?
- Are you giving yourself enough time and space to simply feel and be?
- What do you need to do to feel the way you truly desire to feel?

This is a useful self-audit, encouraging you to tune into and truly listen to your feelings instead of brushing them aside or, worse still, spending hours ruminating on them.

WHAT DO YOU NEED RIGHT NOW?

Whenever I feel a rush of intense feelings, I take time to get out of my overthinking mind, slow down my breathing, and tap into my feeling heart. After a few slow and deep breaths, I ask my heart, *"What do I need right now?"* and whatever the answer is, I gift it to myself. Sometimes it's as simple as a power nap, a pot of tea, a laugh, a good cry, a long walk, or asking someone for help with a challenge. Wherever possible, I love doing this simple exercise by the ocean. If I can't get to the ocean, I visualise it in my mind's eye and allow all my senses to come into play. I find this a great way to re-establish emotional equilibrium and turn my focus from challenging situations to purposeful solutions. It's especially powerful and important to do this when you feel overwhelmed or indecisive. Some challenges don't have a logical solution so tapping into your heart's intelligence can help you gain clarity and cultivate strength and resilience from within.

> *"What you think, you become. What you feel, you attract.*
> *What you imagine, you create."*
> Buddha

WAVES OF POTENTIAL

*"You and I are all as much continuous with the physical universe
as a wave is continuous with the ocean."*

Alan Watts

Like the endless waves in the ocean, endless possibilities exist in
life. To tap into this potential, we must be willing to take risks,
adapt to change and be open to new experiences. As Professor
Emeritus of Medicine and founder of the Stress Reduction Clinic,
Jon Kabat-Zinn[7] says, *"You can't stop the waves, but you can learn to
surf."* To ride the waves of potential means embracing challenges
and change, developing a growth mindset and, most importantly,
focusing on possibilities rather than limitations. It takes courage,
perseverance and a willingness to embrace the unknown, yet the
rewards can be endless.

"Breathing out,
I feel solid.
The waves of emotion
can never carry me away.
Breathing in,
I am still water."

Thich Nhat Hanh (1926 – 2022),
Vietnamese Buddhist monk, peace activist and author

TIPS TO TAP INTO THE WAVES OF POTENTIAL:

◆ Visualise your desired future and focus purely on the
possibilities rather than the obstacles.

◆ Break your goals into manageable steps and take daily
action on them.

◆ Notice what's working and what's not working –
recognise that setbacks and failure are opportunities to
learn and grow.

- Seek out new experiences, step out of your comfort zone, and try new things to help you achieve your desired future.

- Surround yourself with positive and supportive people who believe in you.

- Stay away from energy drainers and the *"Isn't it awful?"* club – the club of people who only see limitations and obstacles; these types of people are experts at blaming, complaining and justifying why it's not possible to succeed.

"Enlightenment is when the wave realizes it's the ocean."
Thich Nhat Hanh

If the ocean could speak, what would it say to you?

JOURNAL PROMPT

 Waves of Wisdom: three ideas – 'ah ha' moments – you had as a result of reading this chapter.

 Neptune's Trident: three actions you can take from reading this chapter.

 Positive ripples: find three people you can talk to about this chapter to create positive ripples.

In the next chapter, we explore life below the waves and the lessons to be learnt from majestic whales and joyful dolphins.

BELOW
THE
WATER

CHAPTER SEVEN

LIFE BENEATH THE WAVES -
WHALES & DOLPHINS
WISDOM - JOY

"A world without dolphins and whales, isn't much of a world at all."
Ric O'Barry[1], American animal rights activist
and former animal trainer

THERE IS SOMETHING DEEPLY enchanting and mystical about life beneath the waves. For me, the ocean conjures up images of diverse and fascinating creatures that inhabit the water, from tiny plankton to dainty seahorses, majestic whales and magical dolphins. My curiosity to explore such life, specifically whales and dolphins, took me on two magical journeys to two incredible islands, Maui in Hawaii and Bimini in the Bahamas.

This chapter is an invitation to learn more about the time I spent on these islands and a suggestion that whenever you get the chance to go to either or both, you say a resounding "YES!"

IT STARTED IN VAIL

In October 2019, Calin was settled in Steamboat and well enough to take a part-time ski patrol post working on Mount Werner as part of his recovery process. Knowing that Calin was in a good space and place gave me the peace of mind to turn my focus to kick-starting my business again. First on my list was a retreat in Vail, Colorado with Dr. Brian Luke Seaward. The retreat focused on advanced stress management techniques and strategies, and was a great follow-on program from the initial stress management certification I had completed in 2012. After one of the meditations, we were invited to choose an envelope containing a card from a basket and take on the role of guardian for whatever animal was on the card. My card had a photograph of a whale and a calf on it that Luke had taken in Maui. This was my **first message** to connect with whales in Hawaii.

A **second message** for Maui followed within 24 hours of leaving the retreat. I took an Uber from Vail to Boulder where I got chatting to the driver about the retreat and mentioned the whale card. He smiled from ear to ear and proceeded to share his Maui story. A couple of years ago, he had taken a trip to the exact place in Maui where his parents had honeymooned. On arrival, he felt such a deep emotional connection that he called his mum to share how he was feeling. When she told him he was created there, it made complete sense. Tears of connective joy streamed down his face. It made me even more curious about how I would feel on my first visit to Maui. I had already heard people talk about the *"mana of Maui"* and hoped this was something I would experience. In Hawaiian culture, "mana" is a concept that refers to a supernatural force or spiritual power that can exist in people, objects or the environment. It is a fundamental concept in Hawaiian spirituality and is believed to be the source of power and energy that can be harnessed or embodied by individuals, places or things.

I have felt this type of 'at home' and spiritual connection to a place many times in Tibet, Bhutan and Nepal when visiting monasteries and meditating with monks. I have several Buddhas in my apartment. Simply looking at them makes me feel at home and brings me instant calm and peace. I get the same 'at home' feeling whenever I am close to and immersed in the ocean, which is why it's a non-negotiable to live close to the ocean.

Maybe I was a monk and a mermaid in a former life?! A MERMONK!

JOURNAL PROMPT

Have you ever been to a place where you felt such a strong connection that it evoked a rush of emotions, tears of joy and the feeling of 'coming home'?

Take out your journal and make a note of the places and spaces that you have felt this kind of connection. The questions below will help you.

♦ Where were you?
♦ What emotions did you feel?
♦ Was there anything specific you were seeing, hearing, smelling, touching or intuitively sensing?
♦ Who was with you?

The **third message** for Maui came right after my Uber ride. I had booked a consulting session with Sam Horn and within minutes of being with her, we were talking about her involvement in Maui's Writers Conference. This led to a conversation about the thousands of whales that migrate there from Alaska every winter! When I receive three messages about the same topic through books, conversations, movies or the radio, I take it as a sign from the universe that I am meant to action the message. I connected the dots and three years later in February 2023, I found myself in Maui on a *Phoenix Rising and Way of the Water* whale watching retreat, organised and led by the founder of White Wolf Journeys, Robbyne LaPlant[2].

CONNECTING TO ROBBYNE

I was looking for something different to do for my 60th birthday in 2022. Thoughts of a shamanic retreat were floating around my head, so I started googling various options. **White Wolf Journeys**, a spiritual and shamanic practice founded by Robbyne LaPlant, popped up. In addition to soul readings, private retreats and healing sessions, Robbyne leads journeys to sacred sites. The journeys that instantly caught my attention were the ones to Bimini and Maui to connect with dolphins and whales. I sent an email to inquire about the May 2022 trip to Bimini as it was close to my birthday, and I was keen to travel. Bimini was fully booked; however, Robbyne mentioned there would be a journey to Maui in February 2023.

In late December 2022, just before I was taking the group to Antarctica for Christmas and New Year, I received an email to say that two places were available for Maui in February 2023. I had such a strong call to say yes to the opportunity, that I signed up, trusting that three weeks later, when I returned from Antarctica, I would be able to sort out flights, accommodation and car hire.

Less than a month after returning from Antarctica, I took a sixteen-hour flight to Los Angeles followed by a six-hour flight to Maui. Thankfully, Robbyne connected me with three other participants from the trip which instantly solved the challenge of accommodation and transportation. One of the women, Charlene, hired a car and her friend Karen was happy to pick me up at the airport and drive me back to the guest house in Lahaina. When things flow like this, it's a sure sign you are on the right path. I was meant to be in Maui and share lodgings with three new soul sisters: Charlene, Karen and Brenda. Karen was our designated driver and made sure we found all the different meeting places. She always managed to find great places to eat at the end of the day too! Charlene and Brenda had done several of Robbyne's trips before and, along with Karen, they were a great source of wisdom, fun and support.

WHEN THE STUDENT IS READY, THE TEACHER APPEARS

Normally I'm the one creating and leading retreats and trips, so going to Maui as a participant was a welcome treat. I knew that meeting Robbyne was going to be an expansive learning experience, and it was! Meeting her husband Guy and 17 other women from around the world added to the adventure. I instantly felt 'at home' and part of a new, diverse family.

It seems I had been called to the sacred island of Maui by the Nommos. Nommos was a new term I learnt from Robbyne and relates to the star beings who choose to take on a physical expression in the bodies of whales, dolphins and mermaids. They play an important role in the Earth's evolution, as Earth guardians and guides from the Sirian Star system to maintain the biosphere of the earth.

The retreat theme of *Phoenix Rising and Way of the Water* was a perfect combination for me as a water lover and an Aries fire sign. Over the six-day period, we immersed ourselves in the magical mana of the island. Daily meditations, water ceremonies, whale watching, art, card readings, a sunrise walk to the dragon's teeth labyrinth, waterfalls, crystals, oils, volcanoes, Buddha statues, Māori stones, the legendary winding road to Hana and 30 minutes in the world's largest singing bowl, were all part of the experience.

Each experience opened a new level of self-awareness, learning and connection to the land. Being suspended in a hammock above the world's largest singing bowl for 30 minutes with over one thousand frequencies moving through your body is an experience difficult to put into words. I undressed down to underwear and wrapped up in one of the dressing gowns we were given. I loaded the dressing gown's pockets with crystals that I wanted to charge. Once I was cradled and settled comfortably in the hammock, I put on an eye mask to take away all visual stimulation. Within minutes of the session starting, I entered a deep sense of peace and total relaxation. The vibrations passing through my body were out of this world. I felt tingling warm energy ripple through every single cell in my body! I felt super light, joyful and even more connected to myself. I entered a timeless beautiful meditative state of pure bliss and I didn't want it to end! For the rest of the day, I felt energised and light. That night, I had one of the best sleeps of the whole trip.

Spending time on the volcano Haleakalā during the full moon was super powerful. Haleakalā is the place where Madame Pele, the goddess of fire, found the strength to confront her sister and face her greatest fear. I felt Pele's energy was a signal to awaken my awareness even more. To see things as they really are, to initiate change and wake up to my full potential, to be more creative and less reactive. Haleakalā was the perfect place to find our own courage and activate the sand from the beach that we had placed in a small glass bottle with the energy of the volcano.

On the final day of the retreat, some of us continued to Hana and the sacred Pi'ilanihale Heiau. This is the world's Hara Chakra and home to the powerful Piko Stone. Having flown halfway across the world to join the trip, there was no way I was going to miss out on this opportunity!

I was blessed to be able to get a ride with Robbyne and Guy. It was pouring with rain on the day we visited the Piko Stone. Our patience paid dividends when a lull in the rain created an opportunity to stand before it and feel its immense energy; an energy so powerful that I could feel myself going off balance! It was a deeply spiritual and profound experience, and one that is hard to explain. Piko Stones hold great cultural and symbolic significance in Hawaii. They are considered sacred, representing a connection to ancestors and the spiritual world. Under Robbyne's guidance, I approached the stone with a sense of humility and total awe. I was barefoot, grounded and rooted to the land. I felt the energy of the stone reverberate in my chest bringing with it a sense of renewal, healing and an even stronger connection to nature. I stood in silence for a few moments then left a flower as an offering of respect and gratitude.

WHALE WATCHING

As part of the retreat, Robbyne booked two private whale watching charters with the Ultimate Whale Watching Company[3], located in Lahaina's harbour. We took one trip at sunrise and a second one at sunset. This was the first time I had been whale watching and what a place to be for the first time! Both of our trips out on the boat were completely different experiences in terms of the sightings, energy, interaction and messages from the whales. It was a truly captivating experience. The anticipation and excitement of seeing whales in their natural habitat is off the scale. I can remember feeling a profound sense of awe and wonder when we saw the first whale surface. Seeing a mother whale and her calf playing together, witnessing a breach, tail slap, or simply grasping the sheer size and grace of these majestic creatures, is in itself a magical experience. Being on the water and witnessing the beauty of the whales gave me an even stronger connection to nature. It was also a reminder of the importance of protecting marine life.

The major message I took away from the two charters was to be *'seen and heard'* to *'show up and speak up'* – to give nature, water and wildlife a voice, and ECHO the messages I received from the landscape and wildlife. Every time I saw the whales dive deeper, I dived deeper into my heart space. When the whales flapped their flukes or gifted us with a full breach, I thought of ways I could show up more fully and bring attention to the importance of taking care of nature, in particular the ocean and marine life that we continue to spoil, despite all the warnings.

Whales are highly intelligent social creatures and have long been regarded as symbols of wisdom and insight. Their presence is seen as a sign of good fortune and spiritual significance. The phenomena of the whale migration from Alaska to Maui is fascinating. Without a doubt, Maui is the best Hawaiian island for whale watching, with the highest number of humpback whales on the planet during the winter months.

WHALE MIGRATION

Whale migration is a long-distance journey that takes place every year as humpback whales migrate from their feeding grounds in Alaska to their breeding grounds in Hawaii. This migration typically takes place between November and May, with the peak season being from January to March. During the summer months, humpback whales feed in the cold waters off the coast of Alaska, building up their fat reserves in preparation for their long journey south. As winter approaches and the days get shorter, they begin their migration to warmer waters where they will mate and give birth – hence the expression that the waters of Maui become a *'nightclub and a nursery'*!

The exact route from Alaska to Maui can vary from year to year; however, scientists believe that they follow a general path along the West Coast of North America before crossing the open ocean to Hawaii. This epic journey covers thousands of miles and can take several months to complete. This remarkable journey and phenomenon draws visitors from around the globe to spend time in Maui and experience these magical creatures in their natural habitat. Dr. Jim Darling[4] is a marine biologist and a researcher who has studied the migration patterns of humpback whales in the Pacific Ocean, particularly their movements between Alaska and Hawaii. His work has helped shed light on the epic journey that humpback whales undertake. Various researchers and organisations in Hawaii – such as the Hawaiian Islands Humpback Whale National Marine Sanctuary and the Pacific Whale Foundation – have also conducted research on humpback whale migrations and behaviours in Hawaiian waters, contributing valuable data and insights into the movements of whales in the region.

After spending the winter months in the warm waters of Hawaii, the whales begin their long journey back to the colder feeding grounds off the coast of Alaska, usually between March and May. Quite a journey and one that is needed to feed and replenish their energy reserves after months of living off their fat reserves. The return journey is usually much faster than the migration to Hawaii as they don't stop to mate and give birth. What an impressive feat of endurance and navigation over thousands of miles!

MY MIGRATION

As an expat, I can relate to making journeys to places that offer a better chance to thrive. I was 27 when I first left the UK to work in Kuwait. It was a migration and a classic rite of passage.

The term 'rite of passage' was coined and created by Arnold van Gennep (1873 – 1957). He was particularly known for his pioneering work in the field of anthropology. In his work titled *Les Rites de Passage* (The Rites of Passage),[5] he introduces the phrase 'rites of passage' to describe a universal pattern of rituals and ceremonies that mark a significant transition in an individual's or a group's life.

He identified three distinct phases within these rites:

Separation – detaching from one's previous status, social role or identity.

Liminality – the transitional phase where the individual or group is neither fully part of their old identity nor fully integrated into the new one.

Incorporation – where the group of individuals is reintegrated into society with the new status having completed the transition. This phase often involves rituals that welcome them into their new roles or statuses

Simple 'rites of passage' are birth, baptism, coming of age, graduation, marriage and retirement. Stage one of my rite of passage in Kuwait was separation from everything and everyone I knew – leaving the familiar. Stage two was transition – a time of testing, learning and growth. Stage three was my earlier-than-planned return to the UK due to the Gulf Crisis – incorporation and reintegration.

After escaping from Kuwait in August 1990, I needed to find another post quickly. I had abandoned my post in Kuwait and returned to the UK under life-threatening circumstances with only my passport and one change of clothes. I had not planned to live and work in the UK again. However, hanging out at home with my parents, even though it was very easy and comfortable, was not an option. I started to apply for posts. I invested in a new pair of shoes, skirt, blouse and a jacket in positive anticipation of securing an interview. I figured my escape outfit and sportswear would not be suitable for interviews!

I was short-listed for a highly sought-after position as a country club manager in Wilmslow, Cheshire. I am convinced my answer to the question, "What was the reason for leaving your last post?" had something to do with it! My answer was the truth! "I deserted my post due to the Iraqi invasion of Kuwait!"

During the interview, I shared how much I had learnt by working in the Middle East and how some of these lessons would help the club thrive. My ability to be decisive, resourceful and take risks were the exact traits they were looking for as the club expanded to meet the demands of exacting members!

It was interesting to identify and adapt some of the skills from such a challenging experience and apply them to my new job in hand.

JOURNAL PROMPT

- What migration and/or rite of passage stories do you have to share?
- Where did you go?
- What did you learn?
- How did this experience shape you?
- What lessons did you take on and integrate into your next journey?

WHALE WISDOM

*"To have a huge friendly whale willingly approach your boat
and look you straight in the eye is without doubt one of
the most extraordinary experiences on the planet."*

Mark Carwardine, British zoologist

Whales have existed for over fifty million years. They are the Earth's record keepers, possessing extensive knowledge of the past. They are highly intelligent and social creatures associated with wisdom, truth, emotional rebirth, creativity, communication and the importance of listening to one's inner voice. They are literally swimming libraries carrying the history of Mother Earth.

In many cultures throughout history, whales have been associated with spiritual power, intuition and communication. They are majestic, awe-inspiring creatures representing a huge symbol of strength and grace in the vast mysterious world of the ocean. They are intricately linked with the element of water and the emotions. They are revered as powerful totems, spirit guides, shamanic allies, and master navigators and guides to those seeking their wisdom.

Connecting to the whales in Maui offered me more insight into the mysteries of the ocean, the cycles of life, death and rebirth, and my own soul's journey as I ventured on a lifelong quest to navigate my own expansive evolution. Although we didn't get close enough to look into the eyes of a whale, the message I kept getting from them was, *"I see you, I hear you, I feel you."*

WHALE SONGS AND CODES

Whale songs are complex vocalisations produced by male whales, particularly humpback whales, during the breeding season. These songs are made up of a series of repeated patterns or themes that can be heard by other whales over vast distances. Scientists have been studying whale songs for many years and have discovered that they range from low-frequency rumbles to high-pitched squeaks and clicks. Twenty hertz is the normal whale frequency, but blue whales have a 100 hertz frequency.

According to the oceanographer, Dr. William Watkins[6], the frequency of loneliness is 52 hertz. It is a mysterious call that cannot be heard by other whales and the call of what is known as the 'loneliest whale' in the world. The whale nicknamed "52 Blue" was originally discovered in 1989 and has been intermittently tracked by scientists ever since. Its solitary nature baffles marine researchers and its very existence has captured the attention and hearts of millions of people. Its call has been detected regularly in many locations since the late 1980s and appears to be the only individual emitting a whale call at this frequency.

The whale itself has never been sighted,; it has only been heard via hydrophones. Scientists at the Woods Hole Oceanographic Institution have been unable to identify the species of the whale. They speculate that it could be malformed or a blue whale hybrid. The reason for Blue 52's presumed loneliness has nothing to do with the fact that he has always been detected swimming alone. It is because the unique frequency of his call means that other whales cannot pick up on it to respond.

Another interesting fact about whales is that they must be conscious to breathe, meaning they cannot fall into an unconscious state for too long, and therefore never fall completely asleep. This is a reminder for us to be more conscious; to make sure we don't metaphorically *'fall asleep'* at the wheel of our own lives. Rather, we can strive to be *'fully awake'* and make conscious decisions for ourselves and for the planet.

ADVICE FROM A WHALE

- ◆ Explore your options
- ◆ Dive deep
- ◆ Live deeply
- ◆ Be seen and heard
- ◆ Life's a breach
- ◆ Value community
- ◆ Listen to your intuition
- ◆ Respect the power of nature
- ◆ Protect what you love
- ◆ Embrace diversity
- ◆ Go the extra mile

If a whale could speak, what would it say to you?

MESSAGES FROM MAUI

I came away with several messages from Maui that may be of use to you on your own journey of self-discovery. The wisdom and grace of the whales symbolised deep connection, intuition and communication. They reminded me of the importance of showing up and speaking up, to be seen, heard and a force for good.

The waters of Maui were a source of healing, cleansing and renewal; they were a timely reminder to connect with the spirit of water and learn from its natural ability to give and receive, to be soft yet strong. Walking the dragon's labyrinth reminded me of the importance of looking inwards, of setting meaningful intentions and of being present to the messages from each step of the spiral pathway to the centre. The time we spent at the Buddha statue was a reminder to reconnect with the teachings of the Buddha, in particular those of wisdom, courage and compassion. The turtles reminded me to be patient, to be resilient and to cherish the 60 years of my life that had already passed as I moved with more wisdom into the years ahead. The power and transformative energy of the full moon on the volcano reminded me of the creative process of destruction and renewal. A reminder that for new things to be birthed, we need to let go of the old and harness all our energy to create positive changes in our lives and to the planet.

I spent an extra day in Maui after the trip to Hana. I wasn't in a hurry to get back to Los Angeles and take the long 16-hour flight to Dubai. I wanted to sit with the messages and learnings from the magical seven days I had spent with Robbyne and the group, and conjure up a plan to be able to join the trip to Bimini in May!

THE CALL TO BIMINI

At the close of the Maui trip, Robbyne mentioned the trip she was running to Bimini to spend time with wild dolphins at the WildQuest[7] dolphin retreat in the Bahamas. I made a mental note of the dates and started visualising how I could make the trip and take Calin with me.

> *"When you want something,*
> *all the universe conspires in helping you achieve it."*
> Paulo Coelho, Brazilian author and lyricist

BIMINI BLUE DOLPHIN POD RETREAT, MAY 2023

I am writing this part of the chapter from one of the best places in the world to connect with dolphins in the wild. I am on a small mystical island in the Bahamas surrounded by a seemingly endless blue ocean. I am here with Calin, and a group of 17 amazing dolphin-loving men and women led by Robbyne LaPlant.

Bimini is a small island in the Atlantic Ocean. It's home to hundreds of bottlenose dolphins. It's the perfect location for the WildQuest dolphin retreat centre that specialises in responsible and sustainable interactions with the wild dolphins that grace the water. It's my second journey with Robbyne within three months. It's amazing how a soul reading in April 2022 flowed into two journeys: one to Maui and now this one to Bimini. I keep nipping myself to make sure it is real!

Yet again I had been called by the Nommos for more expansive insights. It's a very special trip for several reasons. In addition to the pure joy of swimming with wild dolphins, Calin and I are here to celebrate his five years all clear from stage four cancer and our 15th wedding anniversary!

I instantly feel 'at home' here. Calin and I are up at 6am daily to mark the start of a new day with hot coffee on the deck. As we watch the sunrise, we draw one of the mermaid and dolphin oracle cards I had brought with me to see what messages they have for the day. Every day at around 7am, Robbyne guides us through a series of tai chi moves to open the flow of energy.

At 8am, we tuck into a healthy breakfast prepared by Dipti, one of the WildQuest team. I name her the Breakfast Goddess because she creates a divine spread every morning. Breakfasts are al fresco on the deck with our newly formed pod. After breakfast, we pack our own lunch boxes with scrumptious food prepared by the nutrition goddess, Nikita. Each morning we have a couple of hours to journal, paint or simply relax, before boarding the WildQuest catamaran at around noon.

Over five magical days, we learn to live in tune with nature and become one with the ocean. The ocean has become our school and the dolphins our teachers. We have entered an ancient, sacred and timeless portal where hours felt like minutes, and the heart-opening moments spent with the dolphins become deep healing sessions and reminders of the importance of joyful play, freedom, unconditional love and soulful connections. Every day on the boat is unique. Seven hours of bliss, fresh air, open ocean, dolphins and humans. Learning to live in tune with nature, accepting her invitation to go with the flow. Swimming, snorkelling, daydreaming, relaxing, breathing, being totally present and open to the wisdom, healing, magic, and mystery of the sacred blue waters, once the spiritual centre of Atlantis. In Robbyne's words:

*"Dolphins teach us that when we live in tune with the patterns and rhythm of nature, we learn how to truly be in touch and communicate with **all that is**. We imbue mastery, and the ability to live in harmony with all beings, living without judgement. The waters of Bimini serve as an embryonic fluid for us to tap into the dream we carry as we birth our own magnificence."*

A deeper understanding and respect for nature grows stronger as each day passes. Daily reminders and reinforcement that our survival depends on the survival of Mother Nature and all the species above and below the water.

"Among the sea-fishes many stories are told about the dolphin, indicative of his gentle and kindly nature."
Aristotle (384 – 322 BCE),
Ancient Greek philosopher and polymath

'DOLPHINIZED'

When the dolphins graced us with their presence and invited us into their watery world, we swiftly kitted up with masks, snorkel and fins and made our way into the water from the back of the boat. Sometimes our interaction with them was brief, and the minute we were in the water, they decided to swim off. At other times, they invited us to spend over an hour swimming with them, allowing us to float above them as they dived down for food and then swam back up to be around us. We were able to get close enough to look into their eyes and enjoy their smile.

Dolphins have incredible healing powers that radiate through the water with each combination of clicks. According to marine biologists, there is something about the vibrational energy of a dolphin and its sonar that has a positive effect on our biomolecular structure. Being so close to them, we all experienced a hyper dose of this sonar energy; we were being DOLPHINIZED!

I experienced several magical moments when one or two dolphins came very close to me, made eye contact, smiled and shared a series of clicks as if they wanted to tell me something. In return, I smiled and sent beams of loving energy out to them from my heart. Every time the dolphins came close, I took the opportunity to look into their eyes again. It is said that when light meets light, the energy is transferred via the eyes; that the eyes are the windows of the soul. Believing this, I smiled with my eyes, mouth and heart, trusting that, even though I had my mask and snorkel on, they could feel and welcome my energy in return for the magical sonar power they radiated.

THE BIMINI ROAD TO ATLANTIS

On day two of our trip, we sailed out to an underwater rock formation near North Bimini. The legend holds that the rectangular limestone blocks are the path to the lost city of Atlantis, a highly advanced civilisation that suddenly disappeared under water 10,000 to 12,000 years ago. The legend foretells the future rise and rebirth of Atlantis. American clairvoyant Edgar Cayce's prophecy regarding the discovery of Atlantis seemed to come true in 1968 when a private pilot flying over North Bimini spotted this unusual formation of underwater rocks. They appeared to form an ancient road lying in about 15 feet of water just off Paradise Point. The site stretches for about a quarter of a mile. As we snorkelled over this mysterious underwater formation, I was filled with a sense of awe and spiritual connection to rocks. I felt my whole body vibrating with energy as if I was being infused with the myth and wisdom of this legendary lost city, Atlantis. What did the rocks want me to know? I sensed it was a call to echo the importance of environmental stewardship, the need for balance and harmony, and the importance of wisdom and knowledge.

MESSAGES

The message from the whales in Maui was repeated by the dolphins in Bimini: *"I see you, I hear you, I feel you."*

The other clear message I received from the dolphins was to flip out of my overthinking head into my feeling heart; to flip out of stagnation through joyful play in water. To be more of a human 'being' than a human 'doing'. To drift, float, swim, flip and twirl in the water, look around, have fun, smile, and be happy for no reason. Every day the dolphins showed us the importance of playtime as they surfed the waves and circled around each other. They taught us to be present and go with the flow. I didn't have a waterproof camera with me. On reflection, I am glad I didn't. It meant I could focus my attention of being with the dolphins in real-time rather than trying to get the perfect picture of them. They taught us what I heard Robbyne say many times: *"... to be open to the experience, not the expectation of the experience."* Another one of their 'teachings' that Robbyne shared with us was a reminder that *"All that you seek will come to you when you are in a place of joy and gratitude."*

If dolphins could speak, what would they say to you?

DOLPHIN WISDOM

In many cultures and belief systems, dolphins are regarded as sea angels; mighty sacred animals with deep spiritual significance. In native American traditions, dolphins are regarded as powerful totem animals representing joy, harmony and playfulness. In many spiritual traditions, they are seen as messengers of the divine conveying messages of love, healing and protection. They are associated with the concept of rebirth and renewal as they can leap out of the water and transform their environment. In Shamanism, dolphins are regarded as powerful spirit animals that possess healing and transformative powers. They are seen as guides who can help the shaman navigate the waters of the subconscious and access deeper levels of consciousness. Dolphins have been known to assist drowning people and to chase away sharks away from people, so have a well-earned reputation as protectors. The ancient Greeks believed that dolphins carried the souls of the dead to the afterlife and sailors have long believed that dolphins are a good omen.

In Christian artwork, the dolphin is often portrayed as carrying souls to Christ so they can be reborn. They represent self-confidence and strong moral convictions: two attributes that serve us well when it comes to standing our ground and speaking our truth. Like whales, they are a reminder of the interconnectedness of all life. Their joyful interactions with humans and other marine life are a clear demonstration of the importance of living in harmony with each other and our surroundings.

Scan the QR code to see a beautiful video of dolphins in their natural environment.

DID YOU KNOW ....

Five dolphin superpowers I learnt from Nala, the reservation manager at WildQuest:

- **Sleep** – dolphins only shut down half of their brain at a time while the other half remains conscious and takes over all functions. This allows them to rest while staying alert in the ocean.

- **Vision** – besides sonar, dolphins have a panoramic range of visions that allows them to see in two directions at once: above the water and even behind themselves.

- **Super skin** – dolphin skin grows about nine times faster than ours and an entire layer of skin is replaced every two hours, so you won't ever see a wrinkly dolphin! Their skin also secretes a kind of antibacterial gel to deter barnacles and parasites.

- **Empathy** – they are known for rescuing and helping humans and other aquatic species in distress.

- **Healing** – scientists are baffled by dolphins' ability not only to heal quickly but seemingly regenerate missing parts. They won't bleed to death, despite large wounds, as they can constrict blood vessels to stem the flow.

THE DOLPHIN HOUSE MUSEUM –
A BRIDGE BETWEEN HUMAN AND DOLPHIN
CONSCIOUSNESS

On day five of our trip, Calin and I decided to take a break from the water and explore Bimini by foot. We had heard about the Dolphin House Museum and wanted to check it out. Ashley Saunders[8], the charismatic owner and creator of the museum, welcomed us to his 'work in progress'. Ashley has been working on the structure and décor of the museum since 1993, using everything and anything he finds on the beach. Sea glass, tiles, bottles, shells, driftwood and hundreds of nautical artefacts are to be found on all three levels of the building. On the rooftop, we found the perfect lookout to the beach and Ashley's Beacon of Hope lighthouse decorated with conch shells. Guest bedrooms were being developed when we visited so if you find yourself in Bimini and enjoy quirky places to stay, then you will love what Ashley has created ,and is creating – a Bahamian National Treasure.

It was hard to leave Bimini. To be honest, coming back into the real world was a bit of a shock to the system. It felt like we had been immersed in a parallel 'blue' world; a magical portal. This is something I experience pretty much every time I come back to the city after being immersed in nature. It feels like walking between worlds, which is why the crossover back takes me a few days to recalibrate. I tend not to connect with anyone for a few days after a big trip so that I can process and integrate all the experiences from the trip before sharing them.

A huge thank you to the WildQuest team: Jwala, Kathleen, Nishant, Mark, Nikita, Dipti, Lisa, Tanmayi, and boat captain Jagna. If you ever get a chance to go to Bimini, **GO!** It truly is a life-changing experience, and the WildQuest team is simply the best.

PARALLELS

In summary, whales and dolphins are magical marine creatures from which we can draw valuable parallels.

Adaptability – whales and dolphins are incredibly adaptable and move effortlessly between environments. Similarly, personal development calls for flexibility and the ability to navigate life's currents.

Embracing Change – whales migrate across vast distances into familiar and unfamiliar territories. Our own growth often involves venturing into unfamiliar territories that open new experiences and opportunities for learning.

Resilience – whales and dolphins encounter challenges, such as ocean currents and predators, yet they persevere. Cultivating resilience in our business, life and relationships helps us bounce forward higher and stronger from setbacks and disappointments.

Communication – whales and dolphins are known for their sophisticated communication abilities of clicks, whistles and body language. This level of sophistication is also crucial to our own personal development.

Active listening – in their social pods, whales and dolphins actively listen to each other and respond to each other's calls. Similarly, attentive listening and response to us and others are critical for success.

Building relationships – whales and dolphins rely on strong bonds within their pods. Healthy relationships between family, friends and mentors provides encouragement and motivation in our own personal growth journey.

Playfulness – whales and dolphins often display playful behaviour. I witnessed this in Maui and Bimini, and took it is a significant message and reminder to be more playful and find the joy in every journey.

WILDFIRES IN MAUI

Just before I sent the first draft of this book for editing, I heard news of the August 2023 wildfires from Karen, one of the women I roomed with in Maui. I looked at the pictures from my February trip and compared them with the devastating images I was seeing through the media. Tears rolled down my face and my heart was aching. It was a very harsh reminder of the destructive forces that continue to shake our planet. I felt blessed that I had been able to experience the magic of Maui yet saddened that most of what I had seen and experienced during my February visit has been destroyed.

My immediate concern was for all the people, animals, ecosystems and the people working to contain the fires. So many people lost their loved ones, their homes and their belongings. Waves of sadness, helplessness and frustration eventually turned to asking what could be done to help. Answers came from Robbyne when I contacted her to make sure she was able to reach her daughter, who lived in Maui. Thankfully, after a frantic 36 hours, she was able to call her daughter and offer comfort from afar.

Days later, a call for worldwide prayers and light for Maui on 23rd August, along with links to donation and funding pages, made it possible to be a very small part of the solution to a very challenging situation.

ADOPT A WHALE

In 2021 I adopted a whale called Salt, considered to be the "Grand Old Lady of the North Atlantic". She was first sighted in 1976 and named because of the white spots on her dorsal fin resembling sea salt. If you would like to adopt a whale, I highly recommend the Ocean Alliance Whale Adoption[9] program.

DOLPHIN PROJECT

The Dolphin Project[10] is a non-profit charitable organisation dedicated to the welfare and protection of dolphins worldwide. Founded by Ric O'Barry on Earth Day, 22nd April 1970, the organisation aims to educate the public about captivity and, where feasible, retire and/or release captive dolphins. The mission of the Dolphin Project is to end dolphin exploitation and slaughter, as dolphins are routinely captured, harassed, slaughtered and sold into captivity around the world – all in the name of profit.

The Dolphin Project works not only to halt these slaughters, but also to rehabilitate captive dolphins for retirement and/or release, investigate and advocate for economic alternatives to dolphin slaughter, and put a permanent end to dolphin captivity.

JOURNAL PROMPT

 Waves of Wisdom: three ideas – 'ah ha' moments – you had as a result of reading this chapter.

 Neptune's Trident: three actions you can take from reading this chapter.

 Positive ripples: find three people you can talk to about this chapter to create positive ripples.

In the next chapter, we explore water's unique presence in the form of snowflakes, icebergs, and the revitalising power of 'fire and ice' therapy.

*"Water will be many things,
but even in all its forms,
it will always be water.
You are my water.
I think I might be yours too."*

Colleen Hoover, American author

WATER'S UNIQUE PRESENCE

CHAPTER EIGHT

SNOWFLAKES, ICEBERGS, FIRE & ICE
INDIVIDUALITY - PRESENCE - REVITALISE

"Let it snow, let it snow, let it snow."
Lyrics by Sammy Cahn,
made famous by American singer, Dean Martin (1917 – 1995)

I HAVE FOND CHILDHOOD memories of playing in the snow, building snowmen and throwing snowballs at my friends and siblings. Snow wasn't always guaranteed at Christmas so whenever it did snow, we stayed out in it as long as we could and, YES, we all did snow angels! Snow brought us a sense of adventure and excitement. I used to imagine what it would like being an Eskimo and have fun trying to build an igloo or snow den. I loved running in freshly fallen snow, sledding down hills and catching snowflakes on my tongue. Even at an early age, I was mesmerised by the unique formation and intricacy of snowflakes. I loved having rosy cheeks and what I used to call a *'snow glow'* created by snowflakes landing on our face and catching the light. We also *'glowed'* with enthusiasm and joy. Great bonds were formed while we played together in the snow. There was something very comforting about being bundled up in winter clothes, hats and mittens.

You know that peaceful feeling you get when it snows? Scientists[1] claim this is because snow absorbs sound and reduces noise pollution. Snowflakes have the power to create peace, quiet and serenity.

Whenever we came in, there was always hot chocolate ready for us and Mum played the song, *Let it snow, let it snow, let it snow!* It was a favourite childhood wintery song – in fact, it still is! How wonderful that this early childhood connection to snow evolved into leading ten dog sledding trips to the Arctic and three expeditions to Antarctica. Lots of snow, huskies, penguins and polar bears!

SNOWFLAKES

"Kindness is like snow; it beautifies everything it covers."
Khalil Gibran

THE BEAUTY OF INDIVIDUALITY

A blanket of snow, yet no two snowflakes are the same! Every snowflake is a one-of-a-kind masterpiece forming intricate and delicate patterns as it falls from the sky. No two snowflakes are alike and no two individuals are alike. You are the only person on the planet with your fingerprints. You are the only YOU that has been shaped by your journey, experiences, perspectives and aspirations. As no two snowflakes are identical, so each person carries a unique set of talents, passions and perspectives that make them special.

When you have the courage to embrace your uniqueness and value your individuality, the world and everyone you impact are all the richer for it. Besides, if we were all the same, it would be boring. I love living in the United Arab Emirates because it is a melting pot for so many different nationalities. This diversity creates a vibrant dynamic social environment where people can learn from different cultural background. Exposure to different perspectives helps broaden one's horizons, challenges one's assumptions and lead to personal growth. I find it intellectually stimulating and personal enriching. Diverse perspectives lead to creativity and innovation.

John Roedel's work includes a collection of poems that focus on the courage it takes to be who we were born to be. He celebrates the beauty in difference!

My love
you are the rarest
wonder the universe
will ever know.

Your life is a song
that will only be sung once.

Every breath you
take makes history.

Don't chase the fake
rainbow of comparison

My love,
be unashamedly yourself

Don't clone your life
own your life.

From the book *Fitting In Is For Sardines*
Printed with permission by John Roedel

There is an interesting contrast between the uniqueness of snowflakes and the pressure of conforming to societal expectations. Snowflakes are appreciated for their individuality; they teach us how to embrace our own unique qualities as a source of strength and authenticity. Being different is a positive attribute rather than a cause for what is referred to as *'imposter syndrome'*. Imposter syndrome is the feeling of inadequacy or the fear of being exposed as a fraud despite one's accomplishments. When you pair this with societal pressures and norms to conform or fit a certain mould to be accepted, it's easy to see why some play down their innate strengths, gifts and talents. Imposter syndrome can be challenged by recognising and embracing one's individuality and by being in environments where you are encouraged to express your individuality without fear.

Marianne Williamson's timeless quote from her 1992 bestseller, *A Return to Love*[2], touches on this fear and encourages us to step into our God-given power.

"Our deepest fear is not that we are inadequate. Our deepest fears is that we are powerful beyond measure. It is our light, not our darkness that frightens us. We ask ourselves, 'Who am I to be brilliant, gorgeous, talented, fabulous?' Actually, who are you not to be? You are a child of God."

Like the snowflakes that create a blanket of beauty, we can only truly blossom when we accept ourselves exactly as our Natural, Unique, Talented Self, or N.U.T.S. as my dear Greek South African soul sister Anna would say!

Take time to consider all your life experiences and how they have shaped the person you are now. When you look in the mirror, gaze into your own eyes for a moment and say, *"I love you"*. Honour and celebrate even the smallest accomplishments in your life. Know that your path may change as you grow and learn more about yourself. It takes courage, patience and perseverance to stay fully true to yourself, your path and your purpose; however, the rewards are well worth it.

"Like the snowflakes, trust when it's time to stay and when it's time to go, knowing that every experience brings change and growth."

Julie M. Lewis

I am the only one in my family that didn't go into the family business of construction, building supplies and plant hire. I used to help in the shop and builders' yard during school and university breaks, but my heart and soul was yearning for a career in health, fitness, travel and adventure. From a very early age, I was clear on my values and have made it my mission to live and work in alignment with them.

To strengthen your sense of self:

- Make choices that align with your values and beliefs.
- Choose what feels right for you rather than what others may expect of you.
- Trust yourself to make the right choices.
- Pay attention to your thoughts and feelings.

JOURNAL PROMPT

Ask yourself:

- What truly matters to you?
- What makes you feel fulfilled?
- What do you love most about yourself?
- What sets you apart?
- How can you truly honour your individuality?
- What are your unique gifts and talents?
- What oughts and shoulds do you need to let go of and exchange for "I chose to/I love to/I have decided to"?

UNITY

*"A snowflake is one of God's most fragile creations,
but look what they can do when they stick together."*

Vesta M. Kelly, American contributor to humour column
'Pepper and Salt', in *The Wall Street Journal*

As snowflakes come together to form a blanket of snow, so it is smart to combine our skills and talents towards common goals and stick together when the going gets tough. Consider collaboration over competition and experience for yourself how much can be achieved when, for example, you form mastermind groups.

When I first started my expedition business in 2003, I knew that I would need support to take it from one or two trips per year to at least eight to make it financially feasible. Initially, a few friends helped by sharing my trips with their contact base until I developed a website and mailing list. I started doing talks at various business groups and sports clubs to build up interest and eventually I was able to get the support of various companies in terms of sponsorship of different products and services linked to my trips. The biggest scoop came when Land Rover Middle East came on board as a vehicle partner providing me with a brand new LR3, PR, marketing and financial support. This took my business to a whole new level.

The African proverb comes to mind:

*"If you want to go fast, go alone.
If you want to go further, go together."*

ICEBERGS

"Icebergs have a unique ability to attract and fascinate people. They are like floating sculptures, each with its own shape, texture, and personality."

Jon Gertner, American journalist and author

RESILIENCE AND ADAPTABILITY

I remember seeing my first real iceberg back in 2012 after crossing the Drake Passage on a ship with a group of clients heading to Antarctica. When the ship's expedition team alerted us to the sighting, I pulled on my warm gear and headed out to the decks with binoculars in hand to see a huge chunk of ice in the middle of the Southern Ocean. It was a complete contrast to the desert sand dunes I was used to seeing in the UAE! My initial reaction was one of sheer awe and wonder. For a while, I was speechless. The sheer size of the iceberg made me feel incredibly small in comparison. I was looking at a frozen giant towering above the waterline, knowing that there was so much more below.

I remember feeling a sense of excitement in witnessing something so unique, knowing that few people have the chance to visit Antarctica. I felt a sense of peace, tranquillity and a profound connection to the pristine nature of the landscape, even though I know it is one of the harshest places on the planet. Adding to the 'awe factor' was the way the sun was catching on the water to create a sea of mesmerising sparkling diamonds – liquid light. I stood on the deck for a long time. This was a magical moment and I wanted it to last. That first sighting inspired a deep sense of reverence for the raw, honest presence and beauty of icebergs.

ICEBERGS' UNIQUE PRESENCE

What you see of an iceberg or glacier is only half the story. Physical reality is the tip of the iceberg. What you see of yourself at surface level is often only half of your story. Have you noticed or experienced that, on the surface, everything looks fine, yet underneath there is a lot going on?!

Awakening happens when we start to look deeper into our nature and stretch our consciousness in the quest for discovery and expansion. Icebergs could be seen as metaphorical wake-up calls to nudge us to go way beyond the surface of introspection and self-examination; to dive into our 'shadows'; the hidden, often unconscious, parts of our psyche. The massive size and hidden depths of an iceberg is a reminder that there is more to us than we consciously recognise. They are powerful triggers for self-reflection. As we wonder what lies beneath the waterline of the iceberg, we wonder what lies beneath our own surface. What aspects are we repressing or denying? As an iceberg melts and reveals more of itself, we can – through the process of exploring our shadow aspects – gradually bring hidden thoughts, emotions and memories to the surface. I do this through journaling, meditation, artwork and, sometimes, dream analysis. In the context of personal growth, integrating our shadow aspects is about achieving balance between our conscious and unconscious selves. An iceberg needs to be in balance and harmony with its submerged parts to maintain stability. Likewise, we need to acknowledge, accept and integrate our shadow aspects to achieve inner harmony and personal growth. Exploring our shadows often involves confronting our fears, vulnerabilities and uncomfortable truths about ourselves. Only by addressing them can we grow and heal.

What's going on deep inside of you? What submerged aspects of your life are being denied or suppressed? How vulnerable are you prepared to be? When I arranged a beta book edit party, I consciously chose to make myself and my manuscript vulnerable by opening up to the input of 17 people. I knew that doing so would bring fresh perspectives and insights to take the book from what I had gauged a level five at the time, to what you now hold in your hands!

As we dive deeper and come to know more of ourselves, we can take things into our own hands to shape and define what changes are needed to truly flourish.

I use the expression *"I'm in iceberg mode"* to let friends and family know that, despite what they see, I have lots of stuff going on underneath and may need some help sorting things out.

When I think of icebergs, I think of presence, self-awareness, resilience and vulnerability.

Presence in terms of truly being in the now, with no thoughts of the past or the future, simply being with what 'is'.

Self-awareness in terms of being aware of the submerged aspects of our personality, emotions and motivations, understanding them, and exploring the best options to activate them through how we show up and everything we say and do.

Resilience in that, like icebergs, we endure harsh conditions and huge changes, yet we find the strength and courage to stand strong and withstand them, as an iceberg withstands the forces of nature.

Vulnerability in that we choose to break free, and open and expose our insecurities and gifts, as an iceberg melts and fragments to reveal its unique beauty and full spectrum of light.

Icebergs face constant changes in their environment, yet they adapt, persist and let go. They play a key role in the Earth's climate system by reflecting sunlight and helping to cool the planet. As they melt, they release fresh water into the ocean, impacting the distribution of heat around the world. As they shed chunks of ice so they can float more freely, so we too must learn to let go of what is weighing us down so we can move with more ease and grace. Despite their fragile appearance, icebergs are incredibly strong. They melt from the bottom and become top-heavy so they start to flip. The smaller they get, the more they flip until nothing is left. Their slow melting process allows them to last for years, representing strength, presence and resilience in the face of change. As they melt, change shape and disappear, it is a reminder of the importance of appreciating every age and stage of our life; of living a full and fulfilling life as we embrace change and personal transformation.

During our Antarctica expeditions, we go Zodiac cruising and can get pretty close to the icebergs. The sheer size and beauty of icebergs leave you in total awe of the intricate shapes, sparkling ice and a surreal spectrum of iceberg blues. It's such a humbling experience to witness the scale of these colossal ice giants. Despite their imposing presence, they exude a sense of calm, presence and tranquillity. Being so close gave us incredible photo opportunities to catch the play of light on the ice, the reflections in the water and, if we were lucky, a penguin or seal resting on the iceberg!

On my most recent trip to Antarctica in 2022, I was on a Zodiac helmed by one of the Oceanwide[3] expedition guides, Daniel Holne, when he radioed into the ship to say he was going on radio silence. He turned off the engine and his radio so we were in complete silence. He encouraged us to close our eyes to cut out all visual stimulation. This was the most magical five minutes for me. I had an out-of-body experience (OBE). I felt as if I had left my body and was floating above my physical surroundings. I felt weightless, euphoric and totally at peace. Time was distorted; I felt it was much longer than five minutes. I could have stayed there for a while longer! My other senses were enhanced: sound, spatial awareness and sixth sense. I was more attuned to the sounds around me, the creaking and cracking of the ice, my breath, the splash of penguins in the water, and the gentle floating movement of the Zodiac. Through this heightened state of awareness 'sixth sense', I felt so connected to the environment. This memory and feeling will be with me for a long time – a lifetime. I can go there in my mind anytime and relive that sense of peaceful oneness.

WHAT LIES BENEATH

Only 10% of an iceberg is visible above the waterline, while the remaining 90% remains hidden beneath the surface. Similarly, each one of us possesses hidden depths, untapped potential and undiscovered talents that others or even we are not aware of. The Iceberg Theory, as coined by the great American author Ernest Hemingway, is a compelling analogy that can be applied to individuals who show a composed surface exterior, whilst concealing their true emotions, talent and inner turmoil beneath. They might be masking their feelings, pain and insecurities to shield their vulnerability. Beneath this surface exterior lies a reservoir of untouched potential, hidden talents and a whirlwind of emotions that, once uncovered, can surprise and inspire those who take the time to explore the depths of their character.

I am conflict-averse and tend to focus on addressing the immediate issue rather than delving deeper in the emotions or grievances around it. I prioritise a diplomatic solution-focused approach and tend to keep my feelings hidden to avoid further escalation. This is like putting a Band-Aid on a major wound. Eventually, the wound opens again. A different and deeper approach is needed. I have learnt to dive deeper and express what I really feel. Sometimes this has backfired on me, yet for the most part, I found that it has helped me build more trust, empathy and understanding in relationships. There is always more to discover beneath the surface!

If an iceberg could speak, what would it say to you?

"We all have our own icebergs.
Most of what we are is hidden beneath the surface."
Kate Morton, Australian author of *The Forgotten Garden*

How many people do you know that are like icebergs? Only letting you see what's above the surface, refusing to let you see what lies below, leaving it up to you to dive deeper with soul-searching questions to find the other 90%?

We often look at successful people and tend to think they have everything under control. Often, there is so much happening below the surface that no one can see. Success on the outside often belies hard work, rejection, doubts, risks, failures, sacrifices, late nights and discipline that lie underneath.

FIRE AND ICE – REVITALISE

Many years ago, I took a DNA ancestry test and discovered that I have 17% Scandinavian DNA. It helped explain why I feel so drawn to the Nordic regions and Nordic practices, in particular hot and cold therapy. I remember my first sauna experience when I was around 14, thinking it was such a great place to 'sweat it out' and stretch out my muscles before plunging into a cold pool.

Sauna and ice baths, also known as "fire and ice therapy", are two of my favourite wellness practices. After a training session, nothing beats sitting in a sauna and alternating it with cold plunge pools or an ice bath! The benefits of this combination include:

- Improved cardiovascular health, blood flow and circulation.
- Reduction of inflammation and alleviating pain.

- Speeded up recovery time by reducing muscle soreness and fatigue.

- Improved mental health by reducing stress, anxiety and depression.

- A boosted immune system, reducing the risk of infection and illness.

- Detoxification – sweating in the sauna eliminates toxins from the body and plunge pools/ice baths help flush out lactic acid and other waste products.

- Increased energy.

- Improved skin, hair and joint health.

- Reduced muscle tension.

I sometimes get lower back pain and find that hot and cold therapy reduces it. This is backed by a study published in the journal, *Physical Therapy in Sport,* titled 'Heat and cold therapy reduce pain in patients with delayed onset muscle soreness', (Yutan Wang et al, 2021)[4]. It showed that a randomised controlled trail alternating hot and cold therapy reduced pain and increased functionality.

For my 60th birthday in 2022, I gifted myself a focused health and fitness program to include weight training three times a week, 12,000 steps daily, four litres of water, daily meditation, a nutrition plan, stretching and three swim sessions in the sea. I am an early bird so needed to find a gym and trainer that could accommodate training sessions at 6am three times a week. I found the perfect place (RightFit) and personal trainer (Ana Monteiro)[5], a few minutes' drive from my home! I started the gym training mid-January with a goal of getting into the best shape ever for my 60th birthday in April. Even though I have a degree in Sports Science and I am more than capable of working out by myself, I found that having a personal trainer kept me accountable and made sure I optimised my time in the gym.

During this time, I came on board as an Ambassador for RESYNC[6], a new specialized wellness clinic close to the gym. After my gym sessions, I walked over to RESYNC for a three-minute session in the cryotherapy chamber at -110°C followed by a 15-minute red-light therapy. This is a great combination for vascular fitness – the cold causes the blood vessels to constrict to preserve body heat, then the heat from the red light causes the blood vessels to open and flood the body with fresh blood containing nutrients, oxygen and white blood cells, a magical elixir for healing.

One of my other favourite combinations when I am in Steamboat Springs, Colorado is sitting in the hot springs then rolling in the snow. On the last trip to Steamboat, I joined my sister-in-law's daily ritual of immersing her face in a bowl of cold water and ice; a quick and easy facial with 'glowing' results!

JOURNAL PROMPT

 Waves of Wisdom: three ideas – 'ah ha' moments– you had as a result of reading this chapter.

 Neptune's Trident: three actions you can take from reading this chapter.

 Positive ripples: find three people you can talk to about this chapter to create positive ripples.

In the next chapter, we dive into the challenge, journey and transformation process, relating it to my English Channel swim and Mansour Al Dhaheri's Swim 62 challenge.

BE
WITH
WATER

CHAPTER NINE

CHALLENGE, JOURNEY, TRANSFORMATION

*"When you encounter turbulence, choppy waters or setbacks,
it is often a sign that things are about to get wildly better
than they've ever been before."*

Julie M. Lewis

ANSWERING THE CALL

IF ANYONE HAD TOLD ME 40 years ago that I would: leave Sheffield in Yorkshire, the city of my birth and my university, to live, work and marry in the Middle East; escape from Kuwait; be held at gunpoint; manage five-star hotel beach and resort facilities; go on a solo walkabout in Australia for three months; make the cut for the amateur Miss Universe bodybuilding championships; climb several high-altitude mountains; be sponsored by Land Rover; have two Royal patrons for expeditions to Jordan and Morocco; attempt to swim the English channel; meet King Charles III and the President of the United Arab Emirates; sign copies of my first book at the Emirates Festival of Literature; start the first and only women-led expedition company in the United Arab Emirates; lead more than 70 expeditions around the globe, including ten to the Arctic and three to Antarctica; and speak on stages around the globe – I would have laughed out loud!

For a new university graduate in Yorkshire, such wildness seemed a million miles away. What I have learned through all these experiences is the power of being clear on what you want, eliminating all other distractions, and taking action every day towards your dreams and aspirations. I've also learnt the power of asking for help and having a supportive circle of friends and allies.

Life is unpredictable and circumstances can change rapidly. I find that reflecting your past experiences can help you become more adaptable and flexible in your planning. It allows you to learn from the past, make more informed choices, and set yourself up for success.

Taking time out to reflect can be useful when you are planning your next move. Simply create a timeline starting from an age in your life that you choose. Note down any specific challenges, successes, people, changes or experiences you had, all the way through to your current age. Reflecting on your past experiences allows you to see the bigger picture and 'connect the dots' and identify any mistakes or missteps you may have made. This level of self-awareness is crucial for personal growth. It helps you recognise patterns or trends in your behaviour, decision-making and outcomes. Recognising these patterns can help you make more informed decisions. Looking back on your achievements and success can help boost your confidence and motivation.

I am sharing some of my wildest dreams not to boast, but to impress upon you that, in the words of Paulo Coelho, *"If you are brave enough to say goodbye, life will reward you with a new hello."*

I was brave.
I am brave.
You are brave too.

Forty years later, at the tender age of sixty-one when most people are making plans to retire, I am currently 're-firing'! I am open to another round of breakthroughs and willing to say more goodbyes to make way for new hellos, trusting where they will take me. I am on a mission to make the next four decades of my life the best four decades, inspiring and encouraging as many people as possible to say YES to the adventure of life. The theme of water will be central to my offerings moving forward. Keynotes, TEDx talks, masterclasses, coastal retreats and expeditions in, on, around or even under water. You will find full details of them on my website, www.julie-lewis.com.

As aviation pioneer Amelia Earhart said, *"When a great adventure is offered, you don't refuse it."*

ANSWERING THE CALL

In previous chapters, we took a journey through water as a unique self-reflection and personal growth tool. In this chapter, we are going to dive deeper into the power of answering the call to journey into new places and spaces; and to experience challenges as positive catalysts that have the potential to propel us towards expansive growth and transformation.

When we answer our soul's calling, there is a realm where the ordinary gives way to the extraordinary. Where familiar paths fade into the distance, the compass spins wildly and leads us into uncharted waters that go way beyond the horizon into the depths of our fullest potential and transformation, with a dash of uncertainty and adventure along the way.

TAKING RISKS

Taking risks and choosing to challenge ourselves yields so many benefits. When we step outside of our comfort zone and expose ourselves to new experiences, ideas and perspectives, it's a huge boost to our personal growth and learning. This exposure allows us to learn new skills and acquire knowledge and insights that we might not have otherwise gained. Say YES more and see where it leads you.

Successfully navigating challenges boosts our self-confidence and self-esteem, as well as reinforcing the belief that we can handle future challenges. Sometimes we need to take small steps towards our dreams and test the water. At other times, we need take a leap of faith and *'dive right in'*. I took a leap of faith starting Mountain High back in 2003. It was the first and only female-led expedition company in the United Arab Emirates. It was a steep learning curve and a roller coaster ride at the beginning, but eventually the business became second nature to me. For every bump along the way, I notched up a new level of resilience.

Taking risks teaches us how to deal with uncertainty and setbacks. It builds real-time resilience and enhances our adaptability in the face of change. Challenges often require creative and resourceful problem-solving, so when we push ourselves beyond our usual boundaries, we are forced to think outside the box and come up with innovative solutions to be resourceful. What was once intimidating soon becomes familiar territory, giving us the confidence to tackle even bigger challenges. The sense of achievement when we succeed is fulfilling. On the flip side, the sense of perspective when we don't succeed is a priceless lesson and a step on the path to success.

By venturing into the unknown, we open doors to new connections, experiences and avenues that were previously closed. It requires us to confront our fears and uncertainties. The process of facing challenges and obstacles leads to personal growth which in turn boosts our self-confidence. New experiences and challenges that take us into unfamiliar terrain broadens our horizons and equips us with valuable insights along the way.

Stepping into uncharted waters stimulates our creativity and problem-solving abilities. When faced with unfamiliar situations, we are much more likely to come up with novel solutions and ideas. Venturing into new areas often involves meeting new people and forming new connections – connections that are valuable for our personal and professional growth. The unknown can be unpredictable which means it's a great opportunity to build adaptive resilience that can serve you in all aspects of your life and weather future uncertainties.

From my travels around the globe leading more than 70 expeditions, I can guarantee that I, along with my clients, will have a much broader perspective on life having experienced different people, food, culture and landscapes. It allows us to the see the world from a totally different perspective, often leading to more open-mindedness, empathy and tolerance. It can also prove that what we once thought was impossible or out of our reach is attainable. This alone is so empowering and often encourages us to set higher goals. Trying new things can lead to the discovery of new passions and interests; what was once uncharted waters may become a lifelong pursuit of joy and passion.

The memories created from stepping out of our comfort zone become deeply engrained in our psyche. I can say hand on heart that the times I have felt the most alive are the times when I am leading teams on adventure challenges around the globe, speaking on stages, going to wild places, or being part of a team on a mission to make a difference.

Simply by taking on challenges, we feel more alive as we begin to diminish and overcome fear. It's a very liberating feeling, it's where the magic happens.

INSPIRING OTHERS

Our boldness can often inspire those around us. When I came back from climbing my first mountain to celebrate my 40th birthday, it seemed my courage and determination inspired more women to take their own leaps of faith and pursue their dreams. I know because so many of them contacted me wanting to join the next trip. It gave me the courage and confidence to join forces with my Norwegian soul sister Jannike Moe to take 18 women to Everest Base Camp in 2003 and start my own expedition business the same year. Every expedition, retreat, workshop or keynote presentation I deliver is a positive deposit into my courage and confidence 'account'. When I make deposits into this account, everyone around me benefits. It fuels my passion and gives me even more energy.

CHANNEL SWIM - IN AT THE DEEP END

It is often in the deepest and murkiest of places that transformation occurs. One of my numerous transformations came when I answered the call to take on the hardest and most humbling swim in the world, the English Channel. The idea of swimming what is known as the 'Everest of open water swimming' came to me on my 55th birthday while climbing Mount Kota Kinabalu in Malaysia back in 2017. It was pouring with rain on the summit push and, in true 'Julie' style, I took that as a 'sign' to think about doing a water-based challenge that would stretch me out of my comfort zone.

Have you ever had a random *'out of the blue'* hunch about doing something and then actually acted on it?

In August 2017, I acted upon my 'on the mountain hunch' and signed up with the Channel Swimming Association[1] for a team relay swim slot in the summer of 2018, and was actively looking for five other swimmers to join me. A few months before the date, the swimmers who were planning to join me dropped out one by one for various reasons. What could I do? I either had to go ahead solo or default on the slot and lose the hefty deposit I had already paid.

I decided to step way out of my comfort zone, find a coach and ramp up my training to be able to do the six-hour cold water qualifier swim and see what I could do from there. With only five months to prepare, it was a tall order, considering most swimmers train for two years before attempting a crossing. I believed I could swim for six hours in cold water and by June 2018, I managed to achieve it in Dover under the watchful eye of my coach and ex-marathon swimmer, Loretta Cox.

I remember that day so well. There was a break in the weather and Loretta's husband, Geoff, agreed to be on the kayak in the sea so I could swim to him to refuel every hour instead of coming into shore. This gave me access to Jelly Babies, peaches, chocolate feeds and magnesium tablets as and when I needed them. I swam six one-hour loops around the bay starting from the sailing club down to the eastern ferry wall and back. I followed the buoys along the way. I renamed them based on their colour and size. The small yellow ones were the lemons, the big green one was a pepper, the big red one was a tomato, and the large yellow ones leading down to the ferry wall were the pomelos – this was very appropriate as the sea always seemed to be so rough in this area, meaning I was pommelled! The buoys were my trusty guides. Every time I reached the eastern ferry wall, I knew my mission was to get back to the lemons at the start of the loop where I would be rewarded as above from the support kayak.

I've often been asked what I thought of when I swam for those six hours. My answer was that I had a mental playlist of great songs in my head and several mantras, including *I am an ocean of energy* and *Just keep swimming*.

Completing the qualifier swim was a huge achievement for me. It took me more than an hour to stop shaking when I got out of the water. You can spot a channel swimmer a mile off – the disco shakes, the dry robe, bobble hats, Crocs and goggle marks around the eyes. I celebrated with a massage followed by a big bowl of spaghetti bolognese, chocolate fudge cake, a good night's sleep, and a full English breakfast the following morning! I knew this was the beginning of a long journey ahead.

Two days after I completed the qualifier, I flew to Los Angeles to speak on resilience at the Million Dollar Round Table Conference. My speaking slot was on 18th June and my swim slot was on 22nd August, so it was important to get back to Dover as soon as the conference finished.

When I returned from Los Angeles, my new home was a caravan in Deal, about 20 minutes from Dover. I got lucky as it meant I had the place to myself and was able to cook my own meals and enjoy them out on the deck overlooking the fields. I rented the caravan from Elinor Crockford, whom I met at a Mother's Day afternoon tea at the Best Western Hotel in Dover. I am not a mother; however, the afternoon tea deal was too good to miss and luckily for me, it meant I met Elinor!

My days consisted of training swims every morning and afternoon. When I was not swimming, I was eating, stretching, reading or sleeping. Most of the time, I trained with another swimmer, Steve Chivers, who had been training for two years. His daughter Phoebe came to every training session to support him and taught me a few cool dance moves that helped me warm up after coming out of the water.

About two weeks out from my swim slot, I did a ten-hour training swim which was the most I have ever done in my life. I felt like a fish in a bowl going round and round the bay, stopping for a few minutes every hour to take a feed. The theory was that if I could swim ten hours, I would be able to see France and would be more motivated to swim for another five to seven hours to make it to land.

EMOTIONS AND SLEEP DEPRIVATION

I booked a slot to swim on 22nd August 2018. August is supposed to be a better month for successful swims due to more favourable water temperatures and supposedly calmer water. This was not the case in 2018! The weather and conditions on that particular day were not good. I remember waking up and looking out of the window from my hotel room at around 7:30am and thinking, *'It looks pretty gnarly out there!'*

I was staying at the Best Western Hotel Dover Marina and had a sea-facing room with a balcony. I wrapped up and stepped out on the balcony to get a better feel of the day. The sea looked choppy and the sky was an ominous canvas of black and grey with foreboding rain clouds. I came back in, had a shower, then headed down for breakfast. I sent Eric (my boat pilot) a message to let him know I was up and about and eager to get his thoughts. At around 10am, Eric called to suggest we meet for coffee at the café at the side of my hotel. I knew as soon as I walked in that the swim was a 'no go' and within minutes of joining Eric, it was confirmed. *"Not today, Jules! I will call you when there's a window."*

I remember thinking *'Please let there be a window soon.'* Now the waiting game began. I needed to find some healthy distractions until the day of my swim. The distractions came in the form of long walks, a visit to Dover Castle and a train trip to London to take Calin to the airport for his flight back to Abu Dhabi as he could only stay until 24th August.

I must share with you that there was one big distraction and concern that I could have done without. I was very concerned about Calin. He was meant to be on the boat as support crew for my swim. When he arrived in Dover on 17th August, he was behaving totally out of character and hardly spoke. This 'out of character' behaviour was very noticeable to my friends, Ginny and Jenny, who had come to support me. Both asked *"What's wrong?"* and I had no idea. I remember Calin requesting me to only ask him questions he could reply yes or no to, which was very strange. I wondered if something was wrong at work, if something had happened to upset him, or if he had met someone else and didn't know how to tell me.

The whole time he was with me was very challenging. Knowing what I know now, it was a blessing that my swim didn't go ahead on 22nd August. There is no way he could have been fully present on the boat. The journey to get him to the airport for his flight home on was fraught with stress and unanswered questions.

I knew that when I got back to Abu Dhabi after my swim, we had some serious 'sorting out' to do. Little did I know at the time that he had a brain tumour on the left frontal cortex that was causing all the language and social behaviour issues.

On 26th August, Eric called me with instructions to meet him at the marina at midnight ready to swim. I had hoped it would be an early morning start as I fire on full cylinders in the morning. To stay awake at midnight onwards is a huge challenge for me. I called my swim coach Loretta to let her know that it was all systems go.

We met at the marina just before midnight, loaded up the boat and headed round to the start point. As soon as we got out of the marina, the water became very choppy. When we left the harbour gates into open sea, it got worse – much worse! I soon felt seasick which is not a great start to a channel swim. I remember holding on to the side of the boat praying to the weather and sea gods for calmer conditions. My prayers went unanswered. It got worse!

It got so bad that Eric decided to turn around and head back to the marina. It was another *'no go.'* We unpacked the boat and headed back to Loretta's house. I remember looking at myself in the bathroom mirror thinking *'That was a close call!'*

That night, the sea that I loved so much showed me that it can be wild and treacherous and **ALWAYS HAS THE LAST WORD**. I crashed into bed at around 2:30am and fell into a deep sleep.

The next day at around 10am, I got a call from Eric. I half expected him to say *"Come to the marina at midnight"* but instead he said the weather for the next few days didn't look great, and he suggested I take a break for a couple of days.

TAKE A BREAK

I took Eric's advice to take a break from Dover and booked train tickets up to Yorkshire to visit my parents and stay with them for a couple of days. I arrived around three in the afternoon and got settled. Later that evening, when I was helping Mum out, I heard a huge thump in the living room. I rushed in to find Dad on the floor. He had fallen backwards and just missed the Welsh dresser by a few centimetres. I called my sister Jane, who lived across the road from Mum and Dad, and asked her to call the ambulance and explain what happened so I could stay close to Dad until they came. I sat beside him reassuring him that help was on the way. He was able to talk, and I was relieved to see that there were no broken bones or bleeding.

Within minutes, Jane came across to help settle Mum while I stayed with Dad until the ambulance arrived. The paramedic did a full check-up and said Dad didn't need to go to hospital so helped him up and got him settled in bed. That night, I slept on the sofa in the living room so I could be closer to Mum and Dad's bedroom in case either of them needed help. I hardly slept and remembered thinking that this must be what it's like for parents fretting over their newborns or young kids.

Much to my surprise, the following morning I received a call from Eric at around 9am saying there was a window in the weather and he wanted me to be at Dover Marina by midnight that night for my channel attempt! In a daze, I said yes, then realised that would mean two train journeys and a taxi to get back to Dover.

On reflection, I should have asked to delay for at least one day so I could catch up on sleep and not rush down. Instead, I asked my sister to run me to Sheffield station to catch the train to London St Pancras, where I changed for the Dover train. I arrived in Dover at 3pm and headed to Loretta's house to get things together and try and get some sleep.

We had to call around for a support swimmer and see if we could find someone to take pictures as my original support swimmer and photographer had already left Dover. Loretta started putting a food and drinks bag together, and I sorted my swim gear out before hopping into bed at 7pm in the hope of getting some much-needed rest. I normally fall asleep at around 9:30pm and that's exactly what I did, which meant just two hours later I was woken up by Loretta to say it was time to get a move on! We needed to be at the marina by midnight, ready to go.

The original plan was to swim on a neap tide to take advantage of lower and slower water. I was conscious of the fact that I would now be swimming on a spring tide meaning the water level would be higher and running faster. I was also conscious of the fact that I had not had much sleep.

The drive to the marina was short. Eric, his assistant and the official observer from the Channel Swimming Association were waiting for us. We loaded up the boat and headed round to the start point. Within minutes of arriving, it was time to strip down to my swimsuit, hat and goggles and *'grease up'* with a mix of Vaseline and nappy rash cream – oh, the glamour! Eric positioned the boat and beamed a light across the water so I could swim to shore and stand clear of the water. I was excited and nervous at the same time. I felt a surge of adrenaline as I raised my hand and said *"Ready!"*

It was pitch black and very cold. The start horn sounded and my eyes focused on the beam of light coming from the boat. This was my guiding path until I reached the side of the boat and gave the thumbs up to the official observer and Loretta. Despite poor visibility, the smell of diesel from the boat and the cold water, I felt comfortable. Once I got into a steady rhythm, I started my mental music playlist. I had 21 songs ready to roll. First up was one of my parents' favourite soundtracks, *Can't Take My Eyes Off You* by Andy Williams[2].

In my third hour of swimming, it became clear that the current and tides were far stronger than my arms. I thought I was doing OK; however, I didn't realise that I was being carried sideways and backwards towards Dover Ferry Port, not to France! I was swimming in one of the busiest shipping lanes in the world. Eric decided to call me out based on safety. I knew I could swim for ten hours as I had done it three weeks before in training, so I was devastated to be pulled. I remember treading water for a while and asking if I could keep going. The answer was a resounding NO! Normally I wouldn't take no for an answer. I would bargain for more time. But I knew it was not my time. I had to get out.

The minute I touched the side of the boat, it was game over. Tears of disappointment streamed down my face. A combination of factors made it clear that I had bitten off more than I could chew. I was reminded of the fact that two out of three swimmers don't make it across the channel; that more people have climbed Everest than have swum the channel, and that the average age of a channel swimmer was 36 and I was 56 at the time. Combine that with little or no sleep and the emotional strain I had experienced over the last week leading up to my swim, and I was in an extremely challenging situation.

I still cried.

I cried tears of disappointment, frustration and emotional exhaustion. I got back on the boat, wrapped up to keep warm and sat in a bit of a daze for a while. Eric came over, gave me a hug and reminded me that I had taken on one of the toughest swims in the world with only six months' training under my belt. I felt a mix of emotions – disappointment, sadness, frustration, relief and, eventually, gratitude that I was still alive and kicking. That night, my respect for water deepened.

It seemed to take much longer to get back to the marina. The sea was choppy and there was a cold wind. Eric's boat didn't have a covered area (it was more of a fishing boat) so we were very exposed to the elements. I remember sitting down and hanging on to the side of the boat, wrapped in several layers to keep warm. We got back into the marina at around 6am, unpacked the boat and headed home. A hot shower, breakfast and a deep sleep was much needed.

I slept until 11am then walked to the beach for a swim. It was important for me to get back in the water as soon as possible. The water was calm. It was almost as if she knew I needed to be held for a while to restore my faith in her and in myself. Even though I didn't make it to France, I learnt a lot about myself and a lot more about water.

Rudyard Kipling's poem *If* [3] sprang to mind. It's one my father often referred to and encouraged me to learn off by heart. The lines *"If you can meet with Triumph and Disaster, and treat those two imposters just the same,"* went round and round in my head.

In my heart of hearts, I still believe that, with the right training and support, I can do anything I set my heart and soul to. The reflective question I asked myself was, *"Is it my soul or my ego that wants to swim the channel?"*

Not one to quit, I decided to give it another go a year later, this time as a member of a relay team in July 2019. I didn't even make it in the water for my swim leg, as our first swimmer was unable to complete the required 60 minutes before the next swimmer took over! That night, I decided that I would take a break from swimming and passed on the opportunity to join a team in 2020. It was just as well, as Covid disrupted everything that year and I found myself, like thousands of others, working out how to navigate lockdowns, restricted travel, cancelled expeditions and speaking engagements.

Fast forward to 2022 and thoughts of swimming the channel were long gone and replaced by a new project, 'Sixty Years on the Planet'. This was self-created to celebrate and mark my 60th birthday by setting up several expeditions around the globe. It was time to play outdoors again with amazing teams of clients who, like me, had been chomping at the bit to get back into nature. I was back in my element, taking teams to the Arctic, Antarctica, the Camino, Egypt, Montenegro, and Mount Ararat in Turkey. I was answering my soul's calling to spend time in wild places and spaces with incredible teams and guides. It felt so good to be back on form with successful expeditions.

After the Christmas and New Year 2022/ 23 trip to Antarctica, my thoughts turned towards cracking on with the book you now hold in your hands, and manifesting trips to Hawaii and the Bahamas to connect with whales and dolphins as part of my research. I was back home on 7th January 2023 with a head and heart full of new dreams and plans.

Thoughts of being part of another swim challenge were far away until a phone call from the Chair of the Board at the British Chamber of Commerce, Abu Dhabi, Nick Cochrane-Dyet MBE. He asked if he could pass on my number to Paul Walker of Hintsa Performance[4], who had been brought over from the UK to manage the Swim62 Abu Dhabi[5] project. This was a swimming challenge created by Mansour Al Dhaheri[6] as a personal, team and community initiative.

SWIM62 ABU DHABI

My connection to this challenge was a surprising yet welcome opportunity to be part of the women's team supporting the first leg of the swim. I came late to the table in that the swim was set to take place in early March and I came on board mid-February. It's strange how the universe nudges you into new ventures when you least expect it!

"Set your life on fire. Seek those who fan your flames."
Rumi

I had recently returned from two weeks in Antarctica. After re-adjusting to time and temperature, I arranged to meet up with Paul Walker and Katariina Uusitalo, also of Hinsta Performance. We met in Abu Dhabi to find out more about the project. Within minutes, I said, *"Count me in!"*

"You will either step forward into growth or you will step back into safety."
Abraham Maslow (1908 – 1970),
American psychologist and
creator of Maslow's Hierarchy of Needs

The fact that I had not been swim training for over six months didn't deter me. I was about to meet and be part of the most amazing team of people and become part of the Swim62 family. A family headed by Mansour Al Dhaheri, whose story is a living testament to the human capacity to adapt, endure and evolve.

The Swim62 Abu Dhabi project had three pillars to it:

- First, a successful Guinness World Record attempt for the World's Largest Safety Lesson in February 2023. I was one of the speakers at the event supporting the main safety lesson, delivered by Will Walker of Storm Swimming Academy.
- Second, a 62 km swim around the island of Abu Dhabi in March 2023. I was part of the women's swim team of six: Anna-Liina Blomberg, Asma Aljanahi, Becky Gosney, Kalthoum Almaazmi, Sarra Lajnef, and myself.
- Third, an environmental and sustainability awareness drive to enhance, protect and preserve the mangroves through the planting of mangroves.

In addition to this, Abu Dhabi-based Film Gate Productions created a documentary that was shown in VOX cinemas across the UAE in November 2023 and will feature in several film festivals. The documentary has been pitched to Netflix so you might get a chance to see it on TV.

Mansour kindly agreed to jump on three calls with me and share some of the back story – how it all began, what it took to make the dream a reality, and how successfully completing it made positive ripples on a personal and collective level.

MANSOUR'S STORY

There is something special about reaching the age of 40. It's considered a milestone birthday, a time when we start to think more about what we are doing, why we are doing it and what new paths are calling us.

For Mansour, it was a time to check in with where he was and how he could create his future self with more credibility, leadership and visibility. After losing 20 kg gained during the Covid pandemic, he made a conscious decision to take charge of his health and venture into new sports to take him out of his comfort zone. Already a keen Jujutsu student, he was used to having his ego thrown to the ground, and recognised the need to work on several areas to boost his performance. One of those areas was breathing and he figured the best way to do this would be through swimming.

Despite nearly drowning in his youth when he jumped into a pool to retrieve a football, he took on the challenge of getting back into the pool. Working with Arjuna, his swim coach who he fondly refers to as 'Fish', he started from scratch to build his stroke technique, cardiovascular fitness and water confidence. He recalled how out of breath he was in the first few training sessions. Eventually, a 25-metre swim progressed to 50 metres and each time he headed to the pool, he set the goal of doubling his previous swim. When he reached 500 metres, he challenged his Jujitsu friends to swim 1 km. They rose to the challenge and completed the 1 km then looked on in awe as Mansour carried on to swim 2 km.

Realising he was capable of more, Mansour set himself the challenge of swimming 10 km which is a hefty jump from 2 km! After reaching 7.5 km of his 10 km attempt, he was hungry and thirsty, so he quickly learnt the importance of fuelling performance and getting to know his body better. In his quest to improve, he started looking for role models and found one in Ross Edgely[7] who, at the time, was swimming around the British Isles.

Ross's achievements were a positive catalyst for Mansour's journey. The fact that Ross didn't have a typical swimmer's physique –typical swimmer physiques are tall and lean, with long limbs that can pull a lot of water – yet was still able to train and achieve what he did, inspired Mansour to come up with the idea of creating his own swim challenge around the island of Abu Dhabi. He knew it would be 57 km and figured that if he trained to swim a distance of 7.5 km eight or nine times and worked with the currents and tides, it was possible to create modern-day Emirati swimming history. He shared the idea with his swim coach Fish, his Jujitsu coaches Sid and Faisal, and his physical trainer Tiago, who all offered 100% support.

Now the hard work began and for the most part, it was kept 'hush hush' until a few days before it started. As the most decorated swimmer of all time, Michael Phelps says, *"It's what you do in the dark that puts you in the light."* [8]

TRAINING

Training for the challenge was a mix of pool swims and drills, and specific gym exercise during the week, daily ice baths, and longer sea swims at the weekends. Sometimes the sea swims were aimed at completing a certain distance, others by time, but always choosing segments of the swim to correspond to tidal and current patterns, giving real-time experience of what the actual swim would be like. Getting to know the route by training over the planned segments was part of the success formula.

Three months out from the swim dates, it was clear that training, logistics and planning needed a project management team in place. That's when Paul and Katariina came on board to ramp up the game and manage the back and front end of the project, so that Mansour could focus purely on swimming.

"I had peace of mind that the team had my back, I didn't have to worry about anything, so all my energy and focus was on swimming," he told me.

It was clear from my conversation with Mansour that he had built a resilient mindset; in fact, so resilient that when his left leg and hip went numb after the first five hours of the actual swim challenge, he didn't panic or say a word to anyone! Instead, he focused on his stroke, his right leg kick, and zoned in on the bubbles created by the others swimming with him.

"Because of all the training and awareness of the potential hazards, I was more mentally prepared to handle the numbness; rather than panic, I focused on what I could do."

This is an extremely important point. When you are aware of your strengths and have put in months (in Mansour's case, two years) of preparation, you become mentally resilient – literally nothing can faze you.

When it was time to take the first break from the water, Mansour mentioned the numbness to Paul who swiftly sorted it out with massage and manipulation. Having such support is priceless and is often the difference between success and failure.

Mansour was accompanied by two swimmers who completed the whole distance with him; Portuguese open water swimming champion Vania Neves, and Arjuna Don (Fish), a private family swimming coach based in Abu Dhabi. The route had been planned meticulously to take advantage of the tides and currents across day and night. Swim breaks out of the water were on board a support boat to allow the three main swimmers a chance to refuel.

Teams of support swimmers completed shorter sections of the swim. Mansour was aware that many swimmers could swim faster than him and had the typical swimmer's physique, yet did not have the endurance or had been able to put in the same training hours to swim the whole distance of 62 km.

INTERESTING FACTS & FIGURES OF SWIM62:

- Mansour started swimming two years ago
- In 2022, he swam a total of 594 km, which is an average of 11 km per week
- In 2023, in the two months leading up to the event, he swam 290 km, which is an average of 32 km per week

The swim

- During the swim, Mansour covered 62 km
- This is 21,216 strokes
- The swim was 33 hours and 58 minutes from start to finish
- He was in the water for a total time of 18 hours and 53 minutes
- The lap of the island of Abu Dhabi was completed in 29 hours and 37 minutes
- He didn't wear a wetsuit
- He took breaks to feed every 30 minutes, consuming 200ml of electrolytes and around 25g of carbohydrate
- That is 34 feeding breaks
- He consumed 6.8 litres of electrolytes and 3,400 calories from gels and snacks
- Mansour burned 14,000 calories just from the swimming
- The team took 90-minute breaks every five hours where they ate hot food, pizza and doughnuts
- They also took breaks to pray throughout the mission
- Over the two days, the swimmers only got three hours' sleep; they were swimming until 9pm on the first day and then had to get up and swim again at 3am.

The team

- Three swimmers completed the lap of 62 km
- The Al Jasmi brothers swam the lap as a relay team, with two brothers in the water at a time, completing over 20 km each
- Obaid Al Jasmi's event at the Olympics was 100 m freestyle, but in this event he swam that distance 200 times over
- There were over 50 swimmers who took part in the event, which included a team of 6 women, 14 from the police, 11 from the military, and over 10 friends and family members for the final few kilometres

The distance around the island of Abu Dhabi is 57 km; however, to honour the 62nd birthday of the President of the UAE, H.H Sheikh Mohamed Bin Zayed Al Nahyan, the distance was increased to 62 km by adding an extra loop in.

The whole project concept was powered by a very strong emotional 'why' for Mansour. Through pure grit, hard work and a superb support team, he succeeded and, in fact, exceeded expectations. Mansour's two-year journey from an 'out-of-breath beginner' in the pool, evolved into a finely tuned endurance athlete in open water, ready to take on more challenges, He also put Abu Dhabi on the map in terms of swimming and has inspired others to get active in the process.

When we choose to take the road less travelled in our later years, it's often more challenging to do so because of our responsibilities as a partner, a spouse, a parent and employee. It's easy to lose yourself in work, family commitments, community service and everything that comes with being in your forties and fifties. Many put their dreams on hold with a 'when … then' rationale: "When the kids are older, when the mortgage is paid, when I retire … Then I will …"

It's easy to forget yourself; I know because I have done it. I think we all have at some point in our lives. It takes a lot of courage, discipline and willpower to commit to long hours of training in between work, family, friends and life. When you are not training, you are working, eating, planning or sleeping, with little or no time for anything else.

"Judge your success by what you had to give up in order to achieve it."

The Dalai Lama,
the highest spiritual leader and head of Tibet

When you taste success, it's natural to want more. After I climbed my first mountain, it gave me such a huge boost of confidence that I wanted to climb a mountain every year and take others along with me. I felt I could move mountains and had the drive to start my own expedition business so I could turn my new-found passion into a new career.

Likewise, Mansour experienced the elation of completing the swim and seeing the impact it had on others, the community, and the way he was viewed as a father, an athlete and a citizen. He told me it was about *'putting skin in the game'* i.e. being directly involved in something and being affected by how it turns out. This resonated with me as I believe that if we want certain things to happen, we must make them happen. It is important to exercise our free will, to make decisions and choices, rather than wait for fate to intervene, or count on divine messages to spur us into action. Mansour's story is a classic hero's journey of answering the call to adventure, overcoming obstacles, meeting guides and mentors, putting his new-found skills to the test, rallying support, succeeding, and returning home a hero.

CATCH THE BUBBLES 'TILL THE WHISTLE BLOWS

I asked Mansour if there was one specific moment he remembered from the swim. He told me that the one that stood out was on the last leg of the swim, knowing that he had around 12 km to go to complete the challenge. Instead of focusing on the distance, he switched to tunnel vision mode, knowing that the light at the end of the tunnel was getting closer. At times like this, athletes often go into the 'zone' to focus on one thing: it could be their breath, it could be their stroke. For Mansour, it was bubbles.

"I clearly remember asking the swimmers who had joined me for the last leg to create bubbles with their leg kicks. Bubbles that I could lose myself in by catching them on every stroke all the way to the finish line and the sound of the whistle blowing. All I needed was bubbles. My lips and tongue were swollen, I looked like a puffer fish, and my nose was blocked because of being in salt water for so long. I had reached my mental limit; I didn't ask how far we had to go, I just kept catching the bubbles! I had faith in my ability to complete the swim because of all the planning and training leading up to the swim. This faith was paired with the trust I had in myself and the support team around me."

Being 'in the zone' or an altered state is common in endurance athletes. I can relate to the bubble story, as when I was caught in a mountain storm in Russia, instead of focusing on the blizzard, I focused on the guide's red gaiters and boots in front of me. I knew that if I could still see them, I was going to be fine. I remember repeating mentally in my mind, *'Follow the gaiters!'*

When one challenge is over, the *'What next?'* question often follows! I know because every time I come back from leading an expedition, people say, *"What's next, Julie?"* Most of the time, I have an answer because I have planned out the whole year of challenges. However, sometimes I answer, *"Let's celebrate the one we have just accomplished and wait for a 'sign' for what's next!"*

ACTIVE ABU DHABI

Mansour trained for the next challenge, with plans for a third challenge on the drawing board. Challenge number two took place in November 2023. It was a 400 km row around the borders and islands of Abu Dhabi. In addition to the physical challenge of rowing 400 km with a rowing partner, Mansour and the team visited the islands to share and highlight their natural beauty, archaeology, culture and wildlife. It's clear he has been bitten by the adventure bug and is inspiring others to realise their own dreams, regardless of their age, nationality or gender.

Follow, like and share Mansour's adventures: @active_abudhabi.

NYAD

If you are looking for an EPIC great swim story, then I highly recommend you catch the *Nyad* documentary[9]. It's a true story based on endurance marathon swimmer Diana Nyad[10], who set her heart and soul on doing something that no one had ever done before: swim 110 miles from Cuba to Florida **without** a shark cage.

She first attempted this at the age of 28. Strong currents, bad weather and jellyfish stings prevented her from completing the swim which she abandoned after about 76 miles. Around her 60th birthday, she decided to bring the dream back to life and started training again after a gap of 30 years. The documentary outlines her attempts to make the crossing as she battled storms, sharks, deadly jellyfish – particularly the dangerous Portuguese man o' war – as well as physical and emotional setbacks.

Attempts to make the crossing when she was 61, 62 and 63 were halted for several reasons. Despite this, she refused to give up on her dream. She made her fifth and final attempt at the age of 64.

This time she was determined to succeed and had meticulously planned every single detail of the swim to include a specially designed jelly fish bodysuit and the very best support team who had witnessed her previous failures and were fully on board to make the dream possible.

In September 2013, she made it all the way from Havana, Cuba to Key West, Florida, creating modern-day swimming history. There is a lot more to the story so if you are on the lookout for a classic hero's journey story of real grit, determination and resilience, you are in for a treat.

"Whatever your Other Shore is,
whatever you must do,
whatever inspires you,
you will find a way to get there."

Diana Nyad

Diana carried three poignant messages on her way across this stretch of shark-infested waters, and she spoke them to the crowd in her moment of final triumph:

1. Never, ever give up.
2. You're never too old to chase your dreams.
3. It looks like a solitary sport, but it's a Team.

Scan the QR code to learn more about Diana's journey.

HERO'S JOURNEY &
JOURNEY TRANSFORMATION PROCESS

The hero's journey and journey transformation process are two concepts that fit in well with this chapter as they relate to the challenge/journey/transformation theme. Mansour, Diana and I are living examples of this process. I am sure you are too.

Joseph Campbell's famous theory of the Hero's Journey[11] is a powerful narrative framework that explores the common stages and elements found in many mythological and storytelling traditions worldwide. The Hero's Journey typically begins with a call to adventure, followed by the hero's departure from their ordinary world into the unknown. Along the way, they encounter allies, face challenges, and confront their inner demons. The hero ultimately achieves personal growth and transformation through these experiences and returns to their ordinary world, often with a new-found wisdom or a boon to share with their community. This universal template resonates with audiences because it mirrors the human experience of growth, self-discovery and the triumph of the human spirit, making it a timeless and enduring storytelling archetype.

Classic heroes like Odysseus embarking on their epic quests personify the timeless hero's journey theme, where they face trials, discover their inner strength, and ultimately triumph against all odds.

Odysseus played a crucial role in the Trojan War, where he devised the famous Trojan Horse strategy that helped the Greeks infiltrate and conquer the city of Troy. After the fall of Troy, Odysseus embarked on a long and perilous journey back to his homeland, Ithaca. This journey, chronicled in Homer's *Odyssey*,[12] is filled with adventures, including encounters with mythical creatures like the Cyclops Polyphemus, the enchantress Circe, the Sirens, and the sea monster Scylla. Odysseus is celebrated for his intelligence, cunningness and resilience, which enabled him to overcome seemingly insurmountable challenges on his heroic journey.

JOURNAL PROMPT

- What hero's journeys have you experienced?
- What prompted them?
- Where did you go?
- What did you do?
- What did you learn?
- What obstacles did you face?
- Who did you meet and how did they impact your journey?
- How long did your journey last?
- Did you choose to return, or did you decide to stay and begin a new chapter of your life somewhere else?

The journey transformation process is a similar model for personal and spiritual growth developed by the founder of JourneyPath® Institute, Cat Caracelo[13], centred around the metaphor of a journey. The concept is that every person's life is a journey that unfolds in stages, which can be marked by significant transitions or turning points. This process has seven stages corresponding to a different aspect of the journey; separation, threshold, descent, initiation, integration, illumination and, finally, like the Hero's Journey, ends with the person returning, bringing their new-found wisdom and insights back into the world, serving others or by contributing to the community in some way.

Travelling and embarking on new challenges are powerful and transformative ways to get out of your comfort zone, face your fears and grow as a person. What dreams are ready to be birthed through you? What's meant for you will sometimes feel scary and risky. Ease and calm don't always mean you are on the right path. Make some time to make notes about your dreams and aspirations in your *Uncharted Waters* journal.

- Where will you go?
- What will you do?
- Who can help you?
- What training and resources do you need?
- What's your first step?

Someday and one day are not days in the week! Set the day and date and get started.

Trust your gut; it always knows best and will help guide you in the right direction even when it feels like you're lost.

TURNING YOUR DREAMS TO REALITY

- Set clear goals
- Believe in yourself
- Take consistent daily action
- Embrace failure
- Persistence pays
- Surround yourself with the right people
- Visualise success
- Celebrate milestones
- Triple your self-care

- Avoid comparisons – focus on your progress and growth
- Give it 100%!

*"The biggest rewards usually come from having the guts
and perseverance to create your own path."*

Yung Pueblo

REMEMBER

"The trouble is, you think you have time."

Buddha

When you are born, you come into this world naked with
nothing; when you leave, you leave naked with nothing – only the
memories of a life well lived, the places you went, the people you
loved, the difference you made, or the legacy you left. Our time
on Earth is unpredictable and limited. Whether you succeed in
your endeavours or not, the fact that you had the courage to take
the road less travelled speaks volumes.

*"One day you will wake up and there won't be any more time to do the
things you've always wanted to do. Do it now."*

Paulo Coelho

JOURNAL PROMPT

 Waves of Wisdom: three ideas – 'ah ha' moments – you had as a result of reading this chapter.

 Neptune's Trident: three actions you can take from reading this chapter.

 Positive ripples: find three people you can talk to about this chapter to create positive ripples.

In the next chapter, we explore how to find answers from within and around us through anchors, oracles symbols and signs.

IT'S
A
SIGN!

CHAPTER TEN

ANCHORS, ORACLES, SYMBOLS & SIGNS
ANSWERS FROM WITHIN

I HAVE LEARNED THAT when we muster the courage and confidence to sail into uncharted waters on our journey of self-discovery, we often find ourselves searching for guidance and clarity. The moment we stop listening to doubt and start listening to our soul's quest for growth, expansion and meaning, hidden forces and resources come to reward our bravery. The path may not be easy, yet deep down we know that to not take it is denying ourselves the opportunity to flourish and fulfil our soul's purpose. The intention of this chapter is to share some simple practices to help you stay on track and be open to the messages all around you so that you can access the answers from within.

ANCHORS

Imagine sailing through stormy seas without an anchor to hold you steady…

We have all heard the advice to *'throw away the anchor and set sail'*. I am all for that and have done it several times; however, I have been smart enough to make sure I have a few anchors at my disposal! It's important to have access to anchors when we need a break from being tossed around by the waves of change. This means we can literally ground ourselves and feel a sense of control while we create our next move from a position of strength and stability, versus weak and wobbly.

Sometimes we do need to stay moored in the harbour and stay closer to the challenge and solutions in hand, rather than distancing ourselves from them. Instead of running away from challenges, we can meet them head on, on home ground.

The Zen proverb *"Wherever you go, there you are"*, springs to mind. Wherever you go, you take whatever you are carrying in your head and heart with you. Travel and new environments can give us an *'outside in'* perspective; however, there are times when we need to buckle down, sort things out, recalibrate, then take a trip.

> *"All you need is one safe anchor to keep you grounded*
> *when the rest of your life spins out of control."*
> Katie Kacvinsky, American author of the *Awaken* trilogy

Anchors can take many forms. It could be a best friend, coach, family member or mentor that helps to *'guide and ground'*. Anchors can be physical objects, such as a cherished keepsake, a piece of jewellery passed down through generations, or an actual anchor.

MY ANCHORS

I have a small pewter Viking that my Norwegian adventure buddy, Jannike, gave me that has been around the world with me. I hold it in my left hand when I need an extra dose of courage.

I also have a small dolphin made of malachite that my father-in-law gave me when I was training to swim the English Channel. I call it *"Merdolph"* as it looks like a combination of a mermaid (the fluke) and a dolphin. Malachite is a beautiful green mineral considered as a stone of healing. It is believed to have the power to absorb negative energy from the environment and body, making it a popular choice for amulets and talismans. It's also associated with personal transformation, growth and emotional balance.

I also have a small bronze Quan Yin statue I bought in Hong Kong to remind me of the importance of self-compassion. Quan Yin, also spelled as Guan Yin or Kuan Yin, is a prominent figure in Chinese and East Asian Buddhism, as well as in other East Asian religions such as Taoism. She is often referred to as the *"Goddess of Mercy"* or the *"Bodhisattva of Compassion."* She is a symbol of compassion, kindness and mercy, and is revered for her role in helping alleviate suffering in the world.

Crystals are powerful anchors, particularly during times of change, transition and expansion. I love exploring crystal shops and was delighted to find a special one, Crystals Dubai,[1] in Dubai run by Crystal Bill and his wife. It's the most amazing collection I've seen in a while; I never leave without one or two pieces, and love gifting them to clients on retreats and expeditions as positive anchors.

I have one necklace that was gifted on my 60th birthday that I rarely take off. It's a beautiful piece of layered glass that catches the light and reflects the colours I am wearing. Everyone always comments on it. I could have sold it several times over; however, it's a keeper. I have yet to see another one like it. Thank you, Dani and Ollie, for gifting it to me; it's a *Julie power necklace* and will stay with me until I take my last breath.

Anchors can also be rituals or practices that ground us such as meditation, prayer, spending time in nature, or yoga. These anchors remind us of our values, belief and what matters most. When life gets chaotic, returning to our anchors can help us regain our balance and perspective. After long flights across time zones, my body tends to fall out of sync. To find equilibrium again, I find long, barefoot grounding walks on the beach, cold showers, lots of water, fruits and vegetables, and a deep sleep, are superb grounding rituals.

JOURNAL PROMPT

♦ Who and what are your anchors in your life?

♦ Who are you an anchor for?

♦ What anchoring rituals and practices do you already have in place and practice?

♦ What anchoring rituals and practices will you start TODAY?

Here are a few more of my favourite anchoring rituals that you might like to incorporate into your daily life:

MINDFUL BREATHING

"In the breath, there is the power to calm the mind, heal the body, and find peace within."

Asian wisdom

Take a few minutes each day to engage in mindful breathing. Find a quiet space, sit comfortably and focus your attention on your breath. Breathe in deeply counting to four, hold for a count of four, then exhale slowly for four counts. Do this at least three times and you will soon feel calmer, more grounded and connected to the present. If you can do this by water, even better! There are many other types of breathing to try out; explore them and stick with one or two that work well for you.

Slow, deep breathing activates the body's relaxation response by stimulating the parasympathetic nervous system, which promotes calmness and reduces stress. This can help prepare the body for sleep. A study, published in the journal *Psychophysiology* in 2021, showed that slow-paced respiration (approximately six breaths per minute) can enhance parasympathetic nervous system activity, leading to reduced stress and anxiety levels (Laborde et al, 2021).[2]

Take a moment to breathe consciously and you will be amazed at what you can accomplish.

WATER CONNECTION

Spend at least 30 minutes in, on, around or under water every day; **YES**, every day. Whether it's a shower, bath, picnic by a river, walk on the beach, a swim, collecting shells, or even watering the garden, it will help you feel calmer, centred and connected to your Blue Mind!

MORNING RITUALS

"Morning rituals set the tone for the rest of your day. Choose them wisely."
Julie M. Lewis

Explore different morning rituals that help set up a positive tone and start for the day.

My routine is a 20-minute meditation, 20 minutes of stretching, three rounds of Wim Hoff breathing, followed by sipping on a green tea out on my deck looking out to the ocean and drawing an oracle card. After drawing a card, I journal for 15 to 20 minutes and set a few intentions for the day before heading out for a walk, swim or the gym. I am up at 5am daily and spend the first two hours of my day focusing on my mind, body and spirit. A cold shower after my workout followed by breakfast is the perfect way to start my working day. This routine is not for everyone, especially the night owls! If you are not an early bird, work out a ritual for whatever time you wake up. At the very least, upon waking, say *"Thank you for another day on the planet"*, head to the bathroom, look in the mirror, give yourself a big smile, a high-five and say "I love you!"

Choose one to three rituals to start your day. It can be as simple as a smile and three things you are grateful for. Experiment with movement, meditation and journaling. When I first started meditating back in 2001, I focused on a candle flame. Anytime my thoughts started drifting, I came back to the flame. It's a simple way to get started, as is focusing on your breathe or listening to guided meditations.

Gift yourself at least 20 to 30 minutes (ideally one hour) in the morning to tune into the day before opening emails and phone messages! Starting your day like this has a huge positive impact on the rest of your day.

MINDFUL EATING

"Let food be thy medicine and medicine be thy food."
Hippocrates (460 – 370 BCE), Ancient Greek physician,
known as the Father of Medicine

Eating is an experience to savour. How many people do you know that eat on the move or while they are taking calls, watching TV or answering emails? This can lead to overeating, indigestion and a whole host of issues. Instead, I encourage you to switch off all distractions, chew your food, savour each bite, and appreciate the flavours and textures of your food. Before I eat, I take a minute to say "Thank you" for the food in front of me and silently thank the Earth, the elements and the people that have contributed to my meal.

"Hara hachi bu" is a traditional Confucian Japanese dietary principle. It is practiced as a mindful eating guideline and roughly translates to *"eat until you are 80% full or stop eating when you are 80% full."* People are often conditioned to finish their plates or eat until they're very full, so it can take time to adjust to this more mindful way of eating. The easiest way to start wiring in this practice is to:

1. **Eat slowly – savour each bite.** This gives your body more time to recognise the signals of fullness.

2. **Pay attention to your body.** Listen to your body's signals as you eat. Focus on physical sensations like hunger, satiety and the feeling of fullness. Avoid distractions such as watching TV or using your phone while eating, as this can prevent you from being in tune with your body's cues.

3. **Use smaller plates and utensils.** Using smaller plates and utensils can help you control portion sizes and prevent overeating. Smaller dishes make it easier to visually gauge how much you've eaten.

4. **Take breaks.** Pause during your meal to assess your hunger and fullness levels. Put your utensils down, have a sip of water and check in with your body to see if you're satisfied.

5. **Leave some food on your plate.** Make a habit of leaving a small amount of food on your plate, even if it's just a few bites. This can serve as a visual cue that you're practicing *"hara hachi bu"* and not overeating.

AFFIRMATIONS

"The power of affirmations lies in their ability to transform your inner beliefs, potentially shaping the course of your life."

Julie M. Lewis

An affirmation is a powerful statement that cancels out self-limiting beliefs. They are simple statements that generally start with *"I am"* and are stated in the present tense. They are positive, uplifting and super powerful during moments of stress or self-doubt. Take time to create a set of positive affirmations that resonate with you. Once you have written them down, when you wake up in the morning, go to the mirror, look yourself in the eyes, and repeat your affirmation until you feel it, know it and are it. Some people post their affirmations on the screen of their phone, on the fridge, the bathroom mirror or on sticky notes in their wallet. The more you integrate affirmations, the more you can change your patterns and beliefs. Say and feel your affirmations at least twice a day – first thing in the morning and last thing at night. They can be as simple or extensive as you wish. One of the affirmations shared on a retreat I attended in Maui was, *"I am so happy and grateful that everything is aligned in the immediate now, with all the right people and all the right resources to instantly manifest my desires."*

Does it work? When you do the work, everything works!

PHYSICAL ACTIVITY

"Move your body to get out of your mind;
the path to grounded clarity is through physical motion."
Julie M. Lewis

Get out of your mind and into your body! Whenever you find yourself overthinking, ruminating or spending a lot of time in the past or present, it's time to get out of your head!

The fastest way to do this is MOVE your body! Dance, walk, swim, run, shake, do yoga or any form of exercise, and you will soon release built-up tension, be more connected to your body and the present moment. As the American speaker and author Anodea Judith[3] says, *"To lose our connection with our body is to become spiritually homeless. Without an anchor, we float aimlessly battered by the winds and waves of life."* Anodea is known for her work in the field of spirituality, psychology and personal development.

SENSORY GROUNDING

"We all need to get out of our minds at least once a day.
By going out of our minds, we quickly come to our senses."
Alan Watts

We often live life on autopilot as it's a great way to get several things done. However, when we live like this, it's easy to miss out, burn out or simply feel fazed!

When a wake-up call, such as a rogue wave or tsunami, comes along and tosses you out of your boat, the ability to ground is more important than ever. When my father passed while Calin was still undergoing cancer treatment, I truly felt that I had been thrown overboard, mentally and emotionally. Everything was *'up in the air'* and I needed to ground.

When faced with challenging situations like this, simply start to focus on what you can see, hear, feel, smell, taste or intuitively sense. I often use this technique on retreats and expeditions when people need help to ground. I ask them to take three deep breaths, then tell me three things they can see, three things they can hear and three things they can touch or move (it can be three parts of their body). It's a super-fast and simple way to come back to yourself.

Music can also be a very powerful and positive anchor for people. A positive anchor is a psychological concept that refers to a stimulus or trigger that helps a person access a specific emotional or mental state. Music has the power to regulate our mood and emotions. Uplifting or soothing music is a great way to de-stress and create a positive emotional mood. When I was writing this book, I tuned into Keane Wang's albums inspired by water, *Pacific Lull* and *Atlantis*. Keane Wang[4] is a solo pianist based in London.

Keane Wang has kindly given me permission to include a link to soundtracks from his album *Pacific Lull*. Scan the QR code below.

So many other songs have been inspired by water. Here are a few of that I am sure you will know:

- *Bridge over Troubled Water* by Simon & Garfunkel
- *Sailing* by Christopher Cross

- *The River* by Bruce Springsteen
- *Smoke on the Water* by Deep Purple
- *Yellow Submarine* by The Beatles
- *Sailing* by Rod Stewart
- *Moon River* by Audrey Hepburn
- *Ol' Man River* from the musical Showboat
- *Beyond the Sea* by Bobby Darin
- *Cry Me a River* by Julie London
- *Purple Rain* by Prince
- *Singing in the Rain* from the musical of the same name
- *Water Under the Bridge* by Adele
- *Orinoco Flow* by Enya – this is one of my favourites!

Certain songs or pieces of music are often associated with specific memories or moments in your life. The minute you hear these songs, they can trigger feelings of nostalgia and bring back positive or not-so-positive memories. I like to listen to music as a tool to stay motivated while I am exercising.

Instrumental music is very soothing; it gives me a huge sense of tranquillity and serenity. When I need to energise myself, I switch the music over and dance around the room for a while to break up long periods of sitting.

What type of music do you listen to when you need to calm down, boost your energy or be creative? Have fun by creating playlists, go to musicals, concerts and festivals, and consider learning to play an instrument or joining a choir.

COLOUR

"Life is a great big canvas. Throw all the paint you can at it."
Danny Kaye (1911 – 1987), American actor, singer and dancer

When you can't express what you feel in words, try painting your feelings with colour. Invest in a watercolour set and let your feelings flow though the paintbrush. I have a 'one a day' art book and travelling watercolour set that I take on retreats, which act as a simple prompt to paint one square of page daily with whatever colours I see around me.

Colour is such a positive anchor and has several beneficial effects. Different colours can evoke different emotions, so be sure to surround yourself and wear colours that make you feel good, boosting your mood and overall sense of well-being.

Have you ever noticed that soft blues and greens are often used where relaxation is important, such as bedrooms and spas? These colours evoke calmness and serenity. Shades of blue are often used in offices as they promote concentration, mental clarity and trust. Bright colours can stimulate creativity and motivation – think of art studios and design spaces.

I love all shades of blue, teal and coral. I associate them with positive experiences and emotions. We all have colour preferences and it's interesting to explore the deeper meaning of the colours we chose and are drawn to. Teal, for example, symbolises the infinity of the sky and the sea, which is why you will find these colours in many Buddhist/Tibetan monasteries and paintings.

"Colour, by its mere presence, invites the human spirit to
flourish and blossom in love,
And each colour, in all its different shapes and forms,
Is a constant reminder that you never walk this path alone.
And that colour, like love, is the journey, and the journey itself is home."

Mark Wentworth,
British entrepreneur and founder of Colour for Life

To reinforce the positive anchor effect, be consistent in your use of colours, and pay attention to how you feel when you are surrounded by them. I am the *'woman in blue'*, but what about you? If you want to dive deeper into colour, I highly recommend you connect with Mark Wentworth,[5] the global ambassador for colour. Mark is the founder of Colour for Life, and the creator and developer of the Colour PsychoDynamics method. I have attended several of Mark's workshops during his visits to the UAE and always leave inspired to bring my true colours into play. Pick up a copy of his book, *Add a Little Colour to Your Life*[6] – it's an high-content, easy read and will change the way you think about colour!

LIGHT ON

I have a table lamp that I bought many years ago that is a 'lighthouse' for me. It has a gorgeous driftwood base. The minute I come home, I switch it on. It makes me feel 'at home'. It goes off last thing at night and comes back on first thing in the morning. When it's on, I feel everything will be all LIGHT and all RIGHT! Without knowing it, I have created a *'Hygge'* atmosphere.

Hygge is a Danish concept that embodies a sense of cosiness, comfort and well-being. Lighting plays a significant role in creating a hygge atmosphere within the home. In Denmark, where winters are long and dark, lighting is crucial for creating a warm and inviting atmosphere. Soft, warm and gentle lighting helps counteract the darkness and cold outside, making the indoor space feel snug and comforting. Lighting, particularly soft and warm lighting from sources such as candles and lamps, plays a crucial role in achieving this ambience.

ORACLES - SEEKING GUIDANCE

The word oracle comes from the Latin, oraculum, rooted in the word orare, which means to speak or to pray. Here's what the dictionaries have to say about oracles:

- ♦ A person (such as a priestess of Ancient Greece) through whom a deity is believed to speak, such as the Oracle of Delphi.
- ♦ A shrine in which a deity reveals hidden knowledge or the divine purpose through such a person.
- ♦ An answer or decision given by an oracle.
- ♦ A person giving wise or authoritative decisions or opinions.
- ♦ An authoritative or wise expression or answer.

Oracles have been used throughout history as a means of seeking guidance from the divine. I have several sets of oracle cards that I have purchased over the years. I use them personally and on retreats with clients. There's something enchanting and exciting about being open to the guidance and wisdom from pictures, words and card themes. Whether you choose cards yourself or have a session with a card reader, you can begin to access more expansive perspectives.

Something as simple as journaling can be a powerful oracle. When we put pen to paper and allow words to flow freely, we often uncover insights and solutions that were previously hidden. The act of journaling becomes a conversation from the depths of our own unconscious and consciousness. When I look at my journal at the end of the week, it brings my attention to patterns, themes, word thoughts and feelings that can guide my next moves.

Animals are powerful oracle messengers. I love finding out the significance of certain animals showing up, be it a bird, moose, bear, ladybird, cat, dog, horse, or butterfly. When I was training to swim the English Channel, I had a little yellow fish that used to come and join me on my swims. He always showed up when I was starting to feel tired and would swim right in front of my nose. I forgot I was tired and simply followed him blowing bubbles in the water. After a while, he would go away, only to return when I needed a boost!

On another occasion, I was back at Calin's family home in Steamboat Springs heading out in the car to the gym with Calin when I sensed someone or something else was also out and about. I looked over to my right and saw three moose in the garden: a mama moose and her two young ones. I googled the significance of seeing a moose and this is what came up:

1. **Strength and resilience** to overcome obstacles in one's life.

2. **Connection to nature**, appreciation of beauty and a reminder to spend more time outdoors.

3. **Intuition**. In some Native American traditions, the moose is seen as a symbol of intuition and awareness, suggesting that we need to pay closer attention to our instincts and inner guidance.

4. **Solitude and reflection**, a time to withdraw from the busyness of the world and focus on one's inner thoughts and emotions.

5. **Transition and change**. This was particularly pertinent at the time I saw them.

TURTLE

I run retreats on dhows (Arabic boats) and yachts here in the UAE and overseas. I remember one retreat when I woke up extremely early in the morning and decided to go for a swim. I let the captain know I was off to snorkel and swim. Within minutes of getting in the water, I came face to face with a huge turtle. We looked into each other's eyes for what seemed an eternity. The message she gave me was loud and clear – *"Slow down and be patient!"* (At the time, I was pushing to complete a project!)

JOURNAL PROMPT

- ◆ What oracle messages and messengers have you experienced?
- ◆ Where do you go and who do you turn to when you are seeking divine guidance?
- ◆ When do feel you need a divine intervention?

It's in the WATER. Water is a powerful source of symbolism and inspiration for divination and oracles in various cultures throughout history. Here's a few that are specifically linked to water:

Scrying in water. This is a divination technique where you gaze into a reflective surface, such a bowl of water, a pond or crystal ball. The images or visions that appear in the water are interpreted to gain insight into the future or receive guidance from the unconscious mind. Give it a go! What do you see?

Hydromancy is a form of divination that involves observing patterns and movements in water, such as waves, ripples or the flow of a river. The interpretation of these water movements can provide insights into future events or answer specific questions. Why not try it?

Conchomancy is seashell divination that involves interpreting patterns, shapes and sounds made by tossing or casting seashells. Different shells are associated with specific meaning and the arrangement of shells can be interpreted to provide guidance and answers. If you like this idea, you will love Anne Morrow Lindberg's book, *Gift from the Sea*, as she relates different shells to different stages of a women's life. Read it!

Dowsing with water is a practice where diviners use a dowsing rod or pendulum to locate sources of water underground. The concept of dowsing with water having a direct relationship with our feelings or helping us with life questions is not scientifically supported. Nevertheless, some practitioners claim that it can be used for other purposes, such as seeking answers to personal or life-related questions, as dowsing tools can react to subtle energy changes in response to questions or emotional states. The dowser's subconscious mind may influence the movements of the dowsing tool, providing insights or answers to the questions posed.

Water crystal readings involve observing the formation of ice crystals as water freezes. Proponents of this method believe that the shape and patterns of the ice crystals can convey information or messages about a person's state of mind. Some tarots or water oracle cards incorporate water-themed imagery and are used for intuitive readings related to emotions, intuition and the deep subconscious.

SYMBOLS - THE LANGUAGE OF THE SOUL

Symbols are a universal language that transcends words and speaks directly to the soul. They have the power to convey complex ideas, emotions and concepts with a single image. They could be animals, plants, geometric shapes or specific colours. They can help us make sense of some of the things we don't fully understand about ourselves or the world. The concept that symbols are the language of the soul is deeply rooted in various philosophical, psychological and spiritual traditions. Carl Jung, the Swiss psychiatrist and psychoanalyst, explored this idea extensively in his work on analytical psychology. He believed symbols and archetypes served a bridge between the conscious and unconscious mind, representing universal, innate elements of the human psyche. For Jung, symbols were a means of expressing and understanding the complex, often hidden aspects of the self.

If we keep seeing certain symbols, this is often a message for our soul to help us along our journey. I spent five weeks in Cascais, Portugal, in the summer of 2022. Every day I saw several lighthouses and anchors. I interpreted them as symbols of grounded illumination for my path ahead.

Lighthouses can represent several different concepts:

- Guidance and directions
- Strength and stability
- Perseverance and resilience
- Hope and inspiration

What do they represent for you? Make a note in your journal.

OM

I love the 'OM' symbol. Seeing and hearing it brings me peace and joy. Other powerful symbols for me are Buddhas, dreamcatchers, dragons, phoenixes, crystals, circles, shells, dolphins, keys, angels, hearts, and spirals.

Water is a rich source of symbolism in cultures around the world, representing aspects of life, emotions and spirituality. It's a symbol of faith in the divine. Here are some of my favourite water symbols:

- Waves
- Fish
- Anchor
- Water lily
- Spiral
- Boat
- Raindrops
- Compass
- Snowflake

Waves symbolise the ebb and flow of life and the ever-shifting nature of emotions. They can also represent the power and unpredictability of natural forces.

Fish are often seen as symbols of abundance, fertility and transformation. In Christianity, this fish is a symbol of faith, while in some Eastern traditions, it symbolises enlightenment and wisdom.

The anchor is a symbol of stability, security and being grounded.

The water lily represents purity, enlightenment and rebirth. Its ability to emerge from the muddy waters and produce beautiful blossoms is a lovely metaphor for spiritual growth.

The spiral shape is often associated with water and its constant movement. It symbolises the cyclical nature of life, growth and transformation. Have fun looking for and seeing spirals in seashells, whirlpools, and the water spiralling down the drain during your shower or after a bath.

The boat symbolises journeys – real and metaphorical ones. They represent exploration, adventure and the idea of navigating one's life out on the open seas.

The raindrop is a symbol of purity, renewal and cleansing. Rain is a life-giving force that nourishes the Earth and brings new growth. The idea of tears being like raindrops speaks volumes to me in terms of emotional symbolism.

The compass represents a person's sense of direction, purpose or values. The expression 'find my bearings' is a common one when someone is feeling lost or unsure.

The snowflake represents individuality, purity, the fragility of life, winter holidays and transformation.

JOURNAL PROMPT

- ◆ What symbols resonate with you?
- ◆ What do the symbols symbolise for you?
- ◆ When have you felt the power of a symbol in your life and decision-making process?

IT'S A SIGN – NAVIGATING THE PATH AHEAD

If you are looking for a sign, this is it!

If you have ever walked the Camino de Santiago, you will know that the yellow arrows and shells are clear signs you are on the right path. The Camino is a major Christian pilgrimage route with sections running through France, Spain and Portugal. The commonly agreed-upon route for El Camino de Santiago (aka, the Way of St. James) begins at Saint-Jean-Pied-de-Port, France and travels 500 miles through four of Spain's 15 regions, ending at the Cathedral of Santiago de Compostela in Galicia. The trails are not difficult; however, they are long distance (usually 22 to 28 km per day) so require a certain level of endurance and fitness. You can complete the whole trail or do sections of it over a period of time.

I have led two groups on the Camino walk. Each time we have completed 111 km of the route – enough to qualify for a signed and sealed Compostela Certificate. The Chapter of the Metropolitan Church of Santiago continues to issue the certificate. In modern times, the award of the "Compostela" is limited to those who come to the Tomb of the Apostle for religious and/or spiritual reasons, following the routes of the Way of St. James on foot, by bicycle or on horseback.

At the start of the Camino, you are given a Pilgrim Passport which needs to be stamped at least three times per day. The stamps are normally collected at the places where pilgrims sleep, such as hostels, but they can also be obtained in parish churches, monasteries, cathedrals, hotels, town halls and local shops.

The arrows and shells have special significance for all who walk the Camino and play a crucial role guiding pilgrims along this ancient route. The route itself spans various paths, roads and terrains, and it can be challenging without clear markers. The yellow arrows and shells serve as way markers, so you don't get lost – although sometimes you do! Carrying the scallop shell or wearing it as a symbol on clothing or your backpack helps identify pilgrims to locals and fellow travellers.

The Camino is not simply a physical journey. For many, myself included, it's a spiritual one. The yellow arrows and shells symbolise a spiritual path or quest for those seeking a deeper connection with themselves, their faith, or their beliefs. The use of the scallop shell as a symbol pre-dates Christianity and has deep historical and cultural roots. In medieval times, pilgrims would often collect scallop shells from the shores of Galicia, the region where the Camino concludes, and wear them as badges of honour to signify their completion of the pilgrimage.

The arrows and shells foster an incredible sense of camaraderie among pilgrims. It's a symbolic representation of diverse individuals from around the globe all walking the same path, promoting unity and a sense of belonging. Finally, the yellow arrows and shells encourage us to stay present and focus on the path ahead. If you haven't experienced the Camino yet, I highly recommend you plan to do so – if you need any help or would like to join a group, let me know.

Life is full of signs and synchronicities if we are willing to slow down and pay attention. Synchronicity is a concept introduced by Carl Jung. It refers to meaningful coincidences that occur in one's life that cannot be explained by conventional cause-and-effect relationships. It's when two or more events seem to be meaningfully related or connected in a way that goes **beyond** mere chance. Jung suggested that they could serve as messages or signs guiding an individual's journey toward self-awareness and personal growth.

"Coincidences" can contain precious clues about important parts of our lives that need our attention. As we become more aware of coincidences and their meanings, we connect with the an *"underlying field of infinite possibilities, and the spontaneous fulfilment of desire."* (Deepak Chopra, *The Spontaneous Fulfilment of Desire*)[7]

Signs all have a purpose; they can be subtle or glaringly obvious and are there to guide us on our path. If I hear or see something three times, I take it as a sign to action something. Here's one example.

In April 2012, I was flying back to Dubai from Hong Kong. I was watching the movie *Mr. Popper's Penguins*[8] on the in-flight entertainment. The cabin crew came round with hot drinks and a snack which happened to be a Penguin chocolate biscuit! When I got home, I was gifted a book for my 50th birthday, *Things to Do Now You Are 50*. I closed my eyes, held the book in my hand and asked what it wanted me to know. I randomly opened a page, and the sign was loud and clear! It said, *'Go to Antarctica!'* I set about getting a group of women together to do just that and, in December 2012, 14 of us set sail to the ends of the Earth, and we meet lots of penguins! This trip was one of the most rewarding trips I have led and created as it involved the first and only team of breast cancer survivors from the UAE to go to Antarctica.

Magic happens when you heed the signs!
Within the mystery lies the magic.

Water has long been associated with signs in various cultures and belief systems. Think of **rainbows** created by the refraction and dispersion of sunlight by water droplets in the atmosphere. In many cultures, they are seen as signs of hope, promise, blessings and good luck. **Dew** forms when moisture in the air condenses on surfaces during the night. In some cultures, heavy dew on grass or leaves is seen as a sign of good fortune and blessings. It symbolises freshness and new beginnings. **Fog and mist** are seen as signs of mystery, ambiguity, hidden truths and the need to navigate life's challenges with caution. I often feel that the movement of water in the form of ripples or waves is a sign of change and transformation. **Ripples** symbolise that even small actions can create a ripple effect. The way water reflects light can be seen as a sign of inner reflection and self-awareness. LOOK AT WATER closely and see what signs it is offering you (note them down in your journal).

Signs might also come in the form of a chance encounter with a stranger who imparts a piece of timely advice, a book that falls of the shelf and opens to a page with a message for you, or a song on the radio that seems to speak directly to your current situation. These are wonderful messages from the universe pointing us in a direction we may not have considered.

JOURNAL PROMPT

◆ What chance encounters or signs have you acted upon?

◆ What signs did you choose to ignore and why?

◆ When do you feel more drawn to purposefully looking for signs?

Keep a note of all your anchors, oracles, symbols and signs in your journal. Add your thoughts to their significance and meaning.

BE A SOURCE-SEEKER

A source-seeker is someone who actively seeks out knowledge, inspiration and insights from a variety of sources. This can include books, teachers, mentors, codes for life, myths, legends, art, music, a spiritual practice, or simply exploring different philosophies.

How open are you to growth, learning and a willingness to explore new ideas and perspectives? I would like to think of myself as a source-seeker, especially when it comes to seeking out inspiration and insight to fuel my creative endeavours and personal evolution. The source-seeker in me led me to sign up for a transformational nine-week program with the founder of MYSTERYM, Mary-Rita McGuire, as mentioned on page 120.

SYMBOLIC JOURNEYS TO ACTIVATE YOUR IMAGINATION

Mary-Rita is a creative expressive therapist, transpersonal psychology practitioner, certified depth coach, sacred journey process guide and journey path facilitator. She is, in all senses of the word, a source-seeker; a highly qualified and experienced one too!

She kindly agreed to contribute to this chapter with one of the visualisations she guided me through. It is an imaginative symbolic journey to the depths of the ocean where you will discover two items – a sword and a chalice – and explore their personal significance.

Access to the script and the audio file of the guided visualisation is through the QR code below.

Please note: The journey is inspired by Mary-Rita's love for the quest of the Holy Grail as well as the works of Ian Gordon-Brown and Barbara Somers. This includes the book, *The Raincloud of Knowable Things*[9] where you can find the original guided journey.

As you step into the unknown and sail off into uncharted waters, remember to keep your eyes, ears, heart and soul open to the anchors, oracles, symbols and signs that come your way. They might be the very thing you need to guide you through calm and stormy waters. Who knows, they could also uncover hidden treasures within and around you!

JOURNAL PROMPT

 Waves of Wisdom: three ideas – 'ah ha' moments – you had as a result of reading this chapter.

 Neptune's Trident: three actions you can take from reading this chapter.

 Positive ripples: find three people you can talk to about this chapter to create positive ripples.

In the next chapter, we explore water and marine challenges, and how we can take action to resolve them.

"I alone cannot change the world,
but I can cast a stone across the waters
to create many ripples."

Mother Theresa (1910 – 1997),
Albanian-Indian nun

PROTECT
WHAT YOU
LOVE

CHAPTER ELEVEN

POSITIVE RIPPLES - MAKING A DIFFERENCE

*"If all the people of the world can feel love and gratitude,
the pristine beauty of our earth may once again return."*

Dr. Masaru Emoto

WE ARE GETTING CLOSE to the end of our *Uncharted Waters*
journey together. I trust each chapter has brought you even closer
to water and closer to yourself.

My intention is that you feel called and drawn to take individual
and collective action to protect and preserve water so it can protect
and preserve us. It's important to acknowledge the abundance of
water we have in our lives and reflect on the profound gift that it
is. Gratitude for this invaluable resource calls us to be responsible
stewards of its preservation. To protect and cherish waters, is to
honour the sanctity of life itself.

*"Water is a reminder that we are all connected and that our actions
have the power to impact the world in many ways we may not realize."*

Yung Pueblo, poet and *New York Times* bestseller

Beyond gratitude and respect lies the intricate dance of symbiosis – the interdependence that binds us to water, and water to us. Our bodies are comprised of more water than any other substance. Our reliance on water for sustenance, energy and transportation underscores the symbiotic relationship we share.

"Water is the most critical resource issue of our lifetime and our children's lifetime. The health of our water is the measure of how we live on the land."

Luna Leopold (1915 – 2006),
American hydrologist and geomorphologist

The topic of water and life below the water has become more relevant and urgent than ever. At least seven million people lack access to clean water; that is roughly one in ten people on the planet (Water Charity[1]). While the amount of freshwater on the planet has remained fairly constant over time – continually recycled through the atmosphere and back into our cups – the population has exploded. This means that every year, competition for a clean, copious supply of water – for drinking, cooking, bathing and sustaining life – intensifies. Most of the sources of water in rural areas are terribly polluted due to poor sanitation and a lack of waste treatment plants. Overall levels of global pollutants are having a negative effect on the drinking water that is currently clean; as time goes on, this damage will be exacerbated. The Middle East and North Africa (MENA) create immense physical water stress. According to the Water Project[2], the most water-stressed countries are Bahrain, Cyprus, Kuwait, Lebanon, Oman and Qatar.

Solutions to addressing water shortages include dams and reservoirs, rainwater harvesting, aqueducts, desalination, water reuse, and water conservation. The United Nations has long been addressing the global crisis caused by insufficient water supply to satisfy basic human needs and growing demands on the world's water resources to meet human, commercial and agricultural needs. The world has changed and continues to do so at an unprecedented pace. It is estimated that the population will be nine billion by 2050. The burning question is: can the planet and our resources cope with this number of people? In the words of Paul Franklin Watson[3], *"The reality is that if the ocean dies, we die – because the ocean provides all those things which make it possible for us to live on the planet. Over 70% of the oxygen is actually produced by phytoplankton in the ocean, and since the 1950s there's been a 40% diminishment in phytoplankton population."*

Paul Franklin Watson is a Canadian-American conservation and environmental activist, who founded the Sea Shepherd Conservation Society, an anti-poaching and direct-action group focused on marine conservation activism.

When you find yourself saying, *"Somebody needs to do something about this"*, maybe that somebody is YOU! It is clear we need to take individual and collective action to reverse the damage we have done over the decades. Oceans make up 71% of our Earth and provide 50% of the oxygen we need. If the ocean isn't healthy, it's clear that most of our planet will also suffer.

The ocean plays an essential role in climate regulation, providing food, supporting livelihoods and maintaining biodiversity. It plays a crucial role in regulating the Earth's climate by absorbing carbon dioxide and other greenhouse gases. It's an important resource for agriculture, recreation and several other industries, such as coastal tourism, renewable energy, seabed cabling, water desalination and maritime fishing. In addition, it provides a significant source of food for people around the world. This is why we need to protect the ocean and its resources to ensure that we continue to have access to healthy and sustainable food sources.

I recently learned of two interesting environmental stewards, one close to home in Oman and one from Hong Kong where I lived for two years from 2010 to 2012.

HARRY CHAN TIN-MING – HONG KONG'S GHOST NET HUNTER

I heard about Harry[4] through a LinkedIn post by Les Bird[5], a writer, photographer and Board Member of the Royal Geographical Society Hong Kong.

Harry is known as Hong Kong's ghost net hunter. At the time of writing this book, he tells me he will be 71 in June 2024 as well as celebrating his 50th wedding anniversary to Melody. He wants his age to be an inspiration for all, especially for the *"silver hair group"* to find ways to enjoy their retirement with wisdom and experience, and to carry on contributing to the community.

Here is the LinkedIn post by Les Bird that I referred to:

"Ghost nets are fishing nets that have been discarded, lost, or abandoned in the ocean. It is estimated that around 600,000 tons of these ghost nets are generated worldwide every year, and that fishing related plastics make up 46% of the Great Pacific Garbage Patch, which is mostly held together by these discarded nets. Over a decade ago Harry Chan declared war on marine trash and has been working tirelessly to clean up Hong Kong waters of ghost nets. These nets are usually left tangled on a rocky reef or drifting in the open ocean. They can entangle any sea creature, including birds and even the occasional human diver! Commercial fishermen often use gillnets, which are suspended in the sea by flotation buoys along one edge, forming a vertical wall hundreds of metres long, where any fish within a certain size range can be caught. If the net is not withdrawn after use, they continue to trap sea creatures until the weight of the catch exceeds the buoyancy of the floats and the whole thing sinks to the bottom. In time the floats pull the net back up again and the cycle continues. Given the high-quality synthetics that are used today, the destruction just goes on and on."

EHDAA AL BARWANI, OMAN'S MERMAID

Environmentally-conscious mermaid Ehdaa is raising awareness about underwater conservation through photography. The 33-year-old Omani diving instructor is passionate about the ocean and encourages all her students to pick up plastic during their dives. Ehdaa established Aura Divers[6], a pioneering all-women run diving centre, in Muscat in 2022

.

Underwater pictures[7] of Edhaa in her diving gear and traditional Omani clothing are stunning; take a look!

OCEAN BOUND PLASTIC

Ocean plastics represent a major threat to the ecosystem and every living species.

The term *"ocean bound plastic"* was popularised by Dr. Jenna Jambeck, distinguished professor of environmental engineering at the University of Georgia. Ocean Bound Plastic (OBP) is abandoned plastic waste on its way to our oceans and is a critical element in oceanic plastic pollution. Around 80% of the plastic in the ocean derives from this. Plastics that end up near bodies of water, such as rivers, eventually make their way to the ocean. Other plastics reach the sea through storms, sewage systems, ships or offshore platforms. For decades, many countries have dumped waste directly into the sea. This has now been banned in several countries. It's clear that taking care of our water resources and marine life is essential for the health of our planet, along with the well-being of future generations.

Plastic waste represents a huge threat, yet each year, despite conservation efforts, eight million tons of plastic reaches our oceans to join the 150 million metric tons of plastic already there. To create a mental picture of how much plastic ends up in our ocean, imagine a garbage truck dumping its contents into the ocean every minute of the day for a whole year.

The top five trash items found in the ocean are:

- Cigarette butts
- Plastic bottles
- Food wrappers
- Plastic bags
- Straws

The huge challenge is that plastic was built to last. Most items take between 200 to 500 years to break down. Worst still, half of the plastic produced is single-use and only a small percentage of it gets properly recycled; even then, it never really goes 'away.'

Here are a few simple ways that we can take care of the ocean:

1. Reduce single plastic use – this is a major issue harming marine life and polluting the water.

2. Use eco-friendly products, such as biodegradable cleaning products and organic foods that are grown without harmful chemicals which can end up in the ocean.

3. Support ocean-friendly businesses that prioritise sustainability and eco-friendliness.

4. Dispose of waste in recycling bins or a garbage bin. If you see trash on the beach or in the water, pick it up!

5. Volunteer with your local marine conservation organisation.

6. Educate yourself about the importance of the ocean and help spread awareness.

"What we do to the ocean, we do to ourselves."

Dr. Sylvia Earle, American marine biologist
and founder of Mission Blue

HOPE SPOTS

Hope Spots (https://missionblue.org) are special places that are scientifically identified as critical to the health of the ocean. The Hope Spots Map provides an in-depth description of all 140 of the special ocean places identified by Mission Blue[8]. Mission Blue is led by the legendary Dr. Sylvia Earle and aims to unite a global coalition to inspire public awareness along with access and support for a worldwide network of marine protected areas – Hope Spots. Hope Spot status is intended to alleviate the pressures that fishing and drilling place on the ocean, by making the site a higher priority in becoming a marine protected area (MPA), thus forbidding fishing and drilling.

How to Build a Hope Spot

1. Identifying the area – what do you want to protect?
2. Engaging people – who is it critical to speak to?
3. Making the case – what should the proposal contain?
4. Engaging policy – how to get administrations on board?
5. Securing funding – how to achieve sustainable financing?

Inspired by the powerful words of Dr. Earle, Ocean Elders[9] was founded to merge the deep knowledge of scientists with the power of amplifiers; people who could reach broader audiences as well as government and business leaders.

SUSTAINABLE DEVELOPMENT GOALS

The Sustainable Development Goals[10] (SDGs), also known as the Global Goals, were adopted by the United Nations in 2015 as a universal call to action to end poverty, protect the planet and ensure that, by 2030, all people enjoy peace and prosperity.

Of the 17 goals, three specific sustainable goals relate to water and life below the water:

SDG 6 – Clean water and sanitation. This goal aims to ensure universal access to safe and affordable drinking water, improve water quality and increase water-use efficiency in all sectors.

SDG 13 – Climate action. This goal aims to take urgent action to control climate change and its impacts, including the impact of climate change on water resources and marine ecosystems.

SDG 14 – Life below water. This goal aims to conserve and sustainably use the oceans, seas and marine resources for sustainable development.

Sustainable development is an approach that aims to meet the needs of the present generation while preserving the ability of future generations to meet their own needs. It recognises the interdependence between economic growth, social well-being and environmental protection.

"Every positive action creates a ripple of positive change.
It only takes one drop of water to create a ripple; be that first drop!"

Julie M. Lewis

WATER CONSERVATION AND PROTECTION

Clean accessible water for all is an essential part of the world we want to live in. There is sufficient fresh water on the planet to achieve this; however, due to poor economics and bad infrastructure, millions of people die every year from diseases associated with inadequate water supply, sanitation and hygiene. Water scarcity, poor water quality and inadequate sanitation have a knock-on effect on food security, livelihood choices and educational opportunities for families around the globe.

"We never know the worth of water till the well is dry."
Thomas Fuller (1608 – 1661), English historian

Easy ways to help water conservation:

1. Reduce water usage
2. Take shorter showers
3. Only flush the toilet when necessary
4. Limit washing machine use
5. Turn the tap off while soaping your hands or brushing your teeth
6. Collect rainwater to water your garden
7. Fix leaky faucets and use water-efficient appliances
8. Keep pollutants, such as chemicals, pet waste and oils, out of storm drains and waterways, as they can harm aquatic life and make water unsafe for human use
9. Support conservation efforts through donations, volunteering or advocacy
10. Instead of hosing down driveways and sidewalks, use a broom to sweep away debris to avoid unnecessary water usage

CREATE OR JOIN A MOVEMENT

If you care about the planet, you must act. Create one big voice to make some noise by joining or starting a local community group.

Create a monthly beach clean-up or tie in with specific dates linked to water. Myself and a colleague, Maz Wyille, organised a beach clean-up here in Ras Al Khaimah, on World Blue Mind Day (23rd July) that brought the community together to take care of the public beach that is accessible to all. World Blue Mind Day was created by Dr. Wallace J. Nichols and is held annually to celebrate the emotional wellness benefits of time spent near, in, on and under healthy waters.

Stay inspired to be more aware of water in all its forms and create your own ideas and action plans to protect and preserve it. Individual and collective stewardship and action can and does have a positive impact on the larger ecosystem.

BLUE LOVE[11]

By purchasing this book, you are supporting marine conservation, beach and ocean debris clean-ups, coastal and mangrove rejuvenation, and educational talks through Azraq, an organisation I support in the UAE.

AZRAQME.ORG

Azraq[12] was founded by a very dear friend of mine, Natalie Hore (née Banks), as a proactive marine conservation organisation in the United Arab Emirates. I first met Natalie when I took part in a Swim for Clean Seas event in Abu Dhabi organised by Azraq in association with

the Jumeirah Beach Hotel on Saadiyat Island. I was instantly inspired by the event and the work Azraq do, and signed up as an active volunteer.

I Invited the Azraq President and Managing Director, Hala Dahmane, to contribute a few words to this section. It gives me great pleasure to share them here:

"Azraq, a UAE based non-profit organization, is dedicated to protecting and restoring our precious water ecosystems. Its name, which translates into "blue" in Arabic, symbolizes the essence of water itself. Azraq's mission is rooted in the belief that water is not just a resource, but the very source of life.

Through a wide range of initiatives including beach and ocean debris clean-ups, educational talks, mangrove planting and coral restoration, Azraq works to preserve and restore our precious water ecosystems.

Throughout this book, you've witnessed the transformative power of water and the profound lessons it imparts. It is with immense gratitude that I share that Azraq's long-time friend, Julie M. Lewis, the author of this book, has pledged her support to Azraq's projects in and around the UAE. A portion of book sales and royalties will be dedicated to our cause.

These contributions serve as a testament of our shared commitment to creating positive ripples in the world. Let us carry forward the spirit of water – its adaptability, resilience, and life-giving nature – as we ensure the continuous flow of the elixir of life for generations to come.

I extend a warm invitation to you to discover more about Azraq's endeavours and join us in our mission to protect, conserve and rejuvenate the waters of our planet."

JOURNAL PROMPT

- What causes do you feel drawn to?
- Visualize the cause you want to support.
- How can you honour your calling to this cause?

Fill in the following.

I will actively:

1.

2.

3.

BACK TO THE BEGINNING

"Remember you are water and water always finds a way."
Julie M. Lewis

AT THE BEGINNING OF THE book, I asked you to think about what water would say to you if it could speak. I am sure one of the things it might say would be to express concern about how we, as humans, have polluted it and caused environmental damage using chemicals, plastics, waste and overfishing, to name a few. It would ask us for help. It would ask us to use water more wisely and take steps to protect it as a precious resource for future generations. It would ask us to remember that it supports entire ecosystems, and it supports every living thing.

Finally, it would say:

"Without me, there is no life."

Having read the book, what do you think water would say?

In closing…

Embracing water's qualities allows us to flow with the natural rhythms of life, adapting to change and finding greater ease and serenity in every experience. Water's power reminds us that even the most difficult challenges can be overcome with patience, perseverance and adaptability.

When you are looking for answers, look to water.

Be with water.

Be like water.

I truly believe that is where answers lie.

Blue Love,

Julie x

AFTERWORD

PRACTICE BLUE MIND FOR LIFE
DR. WALLACE J. NICHOLS

YOU'VE REACHED THE END of *Uncharted Waters*. And now you are about to embark on your new journey with water.

Julie has given you the gift of a robust, deep, and beautiful toolkit. Activities, meditations, practices, insights, knowledge and wisdom collected over a lifetime. Refer to them often.

We learned in grade school that water is available in three states: solid, liquid and vapour. In the form of snow and ice, lakes and rivers, mighty oceans, fog and clouds.

It also comes to us in seven forms:

- ♦ The wild water that flows and cycles freely.
- ♦ The domestic water that we control temporarily in tubes, tubs, pools, sinks and showers.
- ♦ Urban water in the fountains and waterfronts around our towns and cities.
- ♦ Virtual water in the inspired poetry and prose, music and recordings, artworks, sculptures, paintings, sculptures, photography, or film.
- ♦ Imaginary water that we carry with us everywhere, made of the accumulated memories of sound, colour, light, feel, taste, and smell.

281

♦ The embodied water that makes up most of all living beings, the food we eat, and the nature all around us.

♦ Metaphoric water that can make language, storytelling, creativity, entrepreneurship and communication flow, burst, swell, drift, channelise and splash.

So, what's your water? Make a list of **your** waters in all states and forms.

How can you access your Blue Mind in some way each day, through the ages of your life? Who needs to join you?

Practice Blue Mind daily, for life, wherever you are.

And bring someone who needs it with you.

Photo credit: Rachel Moore

Dr. Wallace J. Nichols
Marine Biologist and Author of *Blue Mind*

Dr. Wallace J. Nichols has authored over 200 scientific papers, technical reports and book chapters, and has lectured all over the world. Dr. Nichols has also been featured in hundreds of print, film, radio and television media outlets.

Formerly a Senior Scientist at Ocean Conservancy, his current focus is on what he refers to as *Blue Mind*, a powerful new universal story of water. His book *Blue Mind* is a national bestseller and has been translated into numerous languages worldwide.

References and Further Reading

Forewatered

1. Dr. Brian Luke Seaward, https://www.brianlukeseaward. com, Paramount Wellness Institute, https://www. brianlukeseaward.com/wp-content/uploads/2020/07/ Advanced-Practices-Level-II-2020.pdf
2. Dr. Brian Luke Seaward, *Stand Like Mountain, Flow Like Water: Reflections on Stress and Human Spirituality*, Health Communications, 2007

Introduction: Moving Mountains to Uncharted Waters

1. Julie Miles Lewis, *Moving Mountains: Discover the Mountain in You*, Panoma Press, 2016

Chapter One: Water, the Healing Elixir of Life

1. Dr. Fereydoon Batmanghelidj, *You're Not Sick, You're Thirsty*, Warner Books (NY), 2003
2. Kangen Water: https://ukkangenwater.co.uk
3. Dr. Masaru Emoto: https://masaru-emoto.net/en/
4. Dr. Catherine Clinton, https://www.drcatherineclinton. com https://www.instagram.com/reel/ C1w67sLrCXd/?igsh=MXRyM2VpY2h5cDBrd

5. Dr. Wallace J. Nichols, *Blue Mind*, Abacus, 2018

6. #bluemindchallenge, World Blue Mind Day. The #bluemindchallenge runs every year from Memorial Day (last Monday in May) to Labour Day (3rd September).

7. Dan Buettner, www.bluezones.com

8. Dan Buettner on Netflix, *Live to 100: Secrets of the Blue Zones*, 2023

9. Dan Buettner, *Blue Zones: Lessons for Living Longer from the People Who've Lived the Longest*, National Geographic, 2009

10. *The Miracle Worker*, 1962, directed by Arthur Penn

CHAPTER TWO: LESSONS FROM WATER

1. Wim Hof, The Iceman, https://www.wimhofmethod.com

2. Alan Watts, *Tao: The Watercourse Way*, Souvenir Press, 2019

3. Dr. Ginny Whitelaw, *The Zen Leader: 10 Ways to Go From Barely Managing to Leading Fear*, Career Press, 2012

4. Dr. Ginny Whitelaw, *Resonate: Zen and the Way of Making a Difference*, Koehler Books, 2020

5. John Roedel, https://www.johnroedel.com

6. C.G. Jung, Richard Wilhem (translator), Cary F Baynes (translator), *I Ching or Book of Changes: Ancient Chinese wisdom to inspire and enlighten*, Arkana/Penguin, 1989

7. *Avatar: The Way of Water*, 2022, directed by James Cameron

CHAPTER THREE: TSUNAMIS, WATERFALLS, RAIN

1. Will Walker, Storm Swimming Academy, https://www.stormswimmingacademy.com

2. Solfeggio Frequencies: https://solfeggioguide.com/solfeggio-frequency-guide/

3. Ultimate Defence Lodge, Nepal, https://www.udnepal.com

4. Tara Brach, https://www.tarabrach.com

CHAPTER FOUR: TEARS, PUDDLES, LAKES

1. Chaplin Robert Orr, Kindred Hospice, Nevada, https://thehazeofgrief.org

2. Paulo Coelho, *The Alchemist*, HarperCollins, 1995

3. Dariush Soudi, Gladiator Mastery program, https://dariushsoudi.com

4. *Dance with My Father*, from the album, *Dance with My Father*, sung by Luther Vandross, written by Luther Vandross and Richard Marx

5. *Dance with my Father* music video, featuring Luther Vandross https://www.youtube.com/watch?v=wmDxJrggie8

6. Robin Sharma, *Who Will Cry When You Die?*, Jaico Publishing House, 2006

7. Robin Sharma, https://www.robinsharma.com

8. *Braveheart*, 1995, directed by Mel Gibson

9. Robert Provine, 2000, 'Laughter – A Scientific Investigation', https://www.researchgate.net/publication/232489851_Laughter_A_Scientific_Investigation

10. Dr Barbara Fredrickson, 'The Broaden-and-Build Theory of Positive Emotions', *Philosophical Transactions: Biological Sciences*, Vol. 359, No. 1449, The Science of Well-being: Integrating Neurobiology, Psychology and Social Science (Sep. 29, 2004), Royal Society, 2004

11. Douglas Adams, Parable of the Puddle, Digital Biota 2 speech, September 1998 https://web.archive.org/web/20160410122229/http://www.biota.org/people/douglasadams/index.html

12. Gerhard Adler & Aniela Jaffé (editors), *Carl Jung, Letters, Vol 1: 1906-1950*, Princeton University Press, 1973

13. Mary-Rita McGuire, MYSTERYM program, https://www.mymysterym.com

14. John Dewy, *How We Think*, Houghton Mifflin, 1933

15.Chris Argyris & Donald Schön, *Theory in Practice: Increasing professional effectiveness*, Wiley, John & Sons Inc, 1974

CHAPTER FIVE: STEAM, STREAMS, SPRINGS

1. Rachel and Stephen Kaplan, *Attention Restoration Theory, The experience of nature : a psychological perspective*, CUP, 1989
2. Harold Dull, **Watsu: Freeing the Body in Water**, Worldwide Aquatic Bodywork Association Publishing, 1993
3. Kelly Howell, The Secret Universal Mind Meditation, https://www.brainsync.com
4. Dr. David Hawkins, *Power v Forces, The Hidden Determinants of Human Behavior*, Unknown publisher, 1985

CHAPTER SIX: RIVER, SEA, OCEAN

1. *The Bridge on the River Kwai*, 1957, directed by David Lean
2. Dr. Deborah Cracknell, *By The Sea: The therapeutic benefits of being in, on and by the water*, Aster, 2019
3. Anne Morrow Lindbergh, *Gift from the Sea*, Chatto & Windus, 1992
4. Joan Anderson, *A Year by the Sea: Thoughts of an Unfinished Woman*, Doubleday, 1999
5. Bernadette Noll, poet, https://www.beachcombingmagazine.com/blogs/news/i-want-to-age-like-sea-glass
6. Mark Anthony, poet, https://www.markanthonypoet.com
7. Jon Kabat-Zinn, *Wherever You Go, There You Are*, Piatkus, 2004

Chapter Seven: Life Beneath the Waves – Whales & Dolphins

1. Ric O'Barry's Dolphin Project, https://www.dolphinproject.com
2. Robbyne LaPlant, White Wolf Journeys, https://www.whitewolfjourneys.com
3. Ultimate Whale Watching Company, https://www.ultimatewhalewatch.com
4. Dr. Jim Darling, www.whaletrust.org
5. Arnold Van Gennep, *Les Rites de Passage* (The Rites of Passage), with Emile Nourry, 1909
6. Dr. William Watkins, https://www.whoi.edu/who-we-are/about-us/people/obituary/william-a-watkins/
7. WildQuest, the Human-Dolphin Connection, https://www.wildquest.com
8. Ashley Saunders, www.dolphinhousebimini.com
9. Ocean Alliance Whale Adoption program, www.whale.org
10. The Dolphin Project, https://www.dolphinproject.com

Chapter Eight: Snowflakes, Icebergs, Fire & Ice

1. University of Kentucky. 'The science behind snow's serenity', *ScienceDaily*, 21st January 2016
2. Marianne Williamson, *A Return to Love*, HarperCollins, 1992
3. Oceanwide Expeditions, https://oceanwide-expeditions.com
4. Wang Y, Li S, Zhang Y, Chen Y, Yan F, Han L, Ma Y. 'Heat and cold therapy reduce pain in patients with delayed onset muscle soreness: A systematic review and meta-analysis of 32 randomized controlled trials'. *Physical Therapy in Sport*, 2021
5. Ana Monteiro, RightFit, https://www.rightfit.ae/team
6. RESYNC, https://resync.ae

CHAPTER NINE: CHALLENGE, JOURNEY, TRANSFORMATION

1. Channel Swimming Association, https://www. channelswimmingassociation.com

2. *Can't Take My Eyes Off You*, sung by Andy Williams, written by Bob Crewe and Bob Gaudio, from the album, Love Andy, 1968

3. Rudyard Kipling, *If* in the book *Rewards and Fairies*, Doubleday, 1910

4. Paul Walker, Hintsa Performance https://www.linkedin. com/in/paul-walker-54336054/

5. Swim62 Abu Dhabi project, https://www.instagram.com/ active_abudhabi/

6. Mansour Al Dhaheri, https://www.instagram.com/active_ abudhabi/

7. Ross Edgley, https://www.rossedgley.com

8. Michael Phelps, https://michaelphelpsfoundation.org

9. *Nyad*, directed by Elizabeth Chai Vasarhelyi and Jimmy Chin, 2023

10. Diana Nyad, www.diananyad.com

11. Joseph Campbell, *The Hero With a Thousand Faces*, Pantheon Books, 1949

12. Homer, *The Odyssey*, Penguin Classics, 2003

13. Cat Caracelo, JourneyPath® Institute, https:// journeypathinstitute.com

CHAPTER TEN: ANCHORS, ORACLES, SYMBOLS & SIGNS

1. Crystals Dubai shop, https://www.instagram.com/ crystalsdubai/

2. Laborde S, Allen MS, Borges U, Iskra M, Zammit N, You M, Hosang T, Mosley E, Dosseville F. 'Psychophysiological

effects of slow-paced breathing at six cycles per minute with or without heart rate variability biofeedback', *Psychophysiology*, 2022 Jan;59(1):e13952. doi: 10.1111/psyp.13952. Epub 2021 Oct 11. PMID: 34633670. https://pubmed.ncbi.nlm.nih.gov/34633670/

3. Anodea Judith https://anodeajudith.com

4. Keane Wang, https://kainbeats.com https://music.apple.com/ae/album/pacific-lull/1697881354

5. https://www.colourforlife.com

6. Mark Wentworth, *Add a Little Colour to Your Life*, Independently published, 2019

7. Deepak Chopra, *The Spontaneous Fulfillment of Desire*, Harmony 2004

8. *Mr Popper's Penguins*, directed by Mark Waters, 2011

9. Ian Gordon-Brown and Barbara Somers, *The Raincloud of Knowable Things: A Practical Guide to Transpersonal Psychology*, Archive Publishing, 2008

Chapter Eleven: Positive Ripples – Making a Difference

1. Water Charity, https://watercharity.com

2. The Water Project, www.thewaterproject.org

3. Paul Franklin Watson, https://www.paulwatsonfoundation.org and ex-Sea Shepherd Conservation Society, https://seashepherd.org

4. Harry Chan Tin-Ming, https://www.linkedin.com/in/harry-chan-tin-ming-陳天明-mh-aba46942/

5. Les Bird, https://www.linkedin.com/in/les-bird-mni-a792711a1/

6. Ehdaa Al Barwani, https://www.auradivers.com

7. https://sekkamag.com/2020/11/24/meet-omans-environment-conscious-mermaid/

8. Mission Blue, https://missionblue.org

9. Ocean Elders, www.oceanelders.org

10. Sustainable Development Goals, https://www.un.org/ sustainabledevelopment/sustainable-development-goals/

11. Blue love is a concept I came up with to embrace water's essence and ignite a passion for spending time in, on, around and under water – for the love of water. Blue love also means supporting water and marine conservation efforts. 10% of royalties from the sale of *Uncharted Waters* and related speaking engagements will be contributed to Azraq to support their beach and ocean debris clean-ups, mangrove planting, coral reef regeneration, and educational sessions for schools.

12. Azraq, www.Azraqme.org

Important Dates

World Whale Day – third Sunday of February: Raising awareness about the conservation of whales, their habitats, and their importance to the marine ecosystem.

World Water Day – 22nd March: Focused on raising awareness about the importance of freshwater resources and advocating for sustainable water management.

National Dolphin Day – 14th April: Dedicated to raising awareness about the conservation of dolphins and their natural habitats.

World Turtle Day – 23rd May: Focused on the importance of protecting turtle species worldwide and their habitats

World Oceans Day – 8th June: Celebrating the role of oceans in our everyday life, and promote the conservation and sustainable use of marine resources.

International Sea Turtle Day – 16th June: Raising awareness about sea turtle conservation and the threats they face in marine environments.

World Seabird Day – 3ʳᵈ July: Highlighting the importance of seabirds and their connection to healthy marine ecosystems.

World Blue Mind Day – 23ʳᵈ July: Created by Dr. Wallace J. Nichols with different themes for each year.

International Whale Shark Day – 30ᵗʰ August: Promotes the conservation of whale sharks, the largest fish species in the world.

Book Club Guidance

Dear Book Club Members,

As you reach the end of this book, I hope the journey through its pages has left you with plenty to ponder and discuss.

To enhance your reading experience, I've included journal prompts throughout each chapter designed to spark thoughtful conversations and reflections during your book club meetings.

I would love to hear about your discussions and thoughts, and I'm excited to explore opportunities to join your group as a guest author. Please don't hesitate to reach out to me with your feedback and to enquire about scheduling a visit via julie@julie-lewis.com

I look forward to sharing more insights and signed books with you all.

Lots of love and water!

Acknowledgements

FIRST AND FOREMOST, my gratitude runs eternally deep to **my late parents, Reginald and Dorothy Vickers**, whose love for each other gave me and my three siblings – Jane, Susan and Paul – the gift of life. All four of us were created out of a magical union of marriage that stood the test of time; 71 years to be precise. We were nurtured and nourished for nine months in our first magical ocean – Mum's watery womb. As young children, we were blessed to spend many summer and Easter breaks on the East Coast of the UK where our love of water began. A love that continues. I know that Mum and Dad are looking over all of us with so much love and pride.

For my husband Calin, who is strong and wise enough to know that every time I set off on an adventure or disappear for a while to write, I am not leaving – I am going to myself. I am going to enjoy stillness, silence and solitude. I am going into nature and to water because it's my food and oxygen! Thank you for understanding that. Our love of nature and each other has taken us around the globe, seeking wild experiences above and below the waves. Long may that continue. I am so happy that your passion for diving and ocean sustainability is now turning into your new vocation.

For my extended soul family: My sisters from other misters and brothers from other mothers – you know who you are! I love you and will always 'have your back'.

For Julie Buck, Leigh-Anne and Chris Price who made it possible for me to have a wonderful *'third place'* to write in one of my new favourite places on the planet: Cascais, Portugal. **For Daisy and Alfie**, my four-legged furry friends in Cascais: we walked along the Atlantic Ocean coast for miles together and many new ideas were born from those walks.

For Sam Horn whose wise guidance continues to inspire thousands of speakers and writers around the globe, myself included. I have fond memories of exploring ideas for this book with you at your home by Wonderland Lake, Boulder, Colorado. Your suggestions of a book edit party was a winner and I literally took it to the water on a yacht with 17 willing beta book readers.

It takes a village and lucky for me I live in one on the slow coast of Ras Al Khaimah in the northern Emirates of the United Arab Emirates. The arrival of two brand new yachts in the marina made it possible to hire one of them and invite 17 beta readers on board for a cruise to read my manuscript and offer their feedback and suggestions. I was told this was a very brave thing to do. It was! It was also a very wise thing to do. My bravery was rewarded with incredible insights and expansive thoughts. Thank you so much: **Tricia, Mary-Rita, Aeron, Mike, Alex, Claire, Michelle, Katherine, Linda, Nigel, James, Alison, Warshi, Evan, Georgina, Michael, and Alex. A super special thank you to Mary-Rita** who offered to take my manuscript home to read it all the way through and offer her thoughts; that's what gifted creative depth coaches do! To **Wendy and Renuka** who couldn't make the boat trip yet took time to look over the manuscript and give feedback. For **Tarek at Skywalker Yachts** and the crew on board the yacht FIBO, Captain Moussa, Anas and Supin, for making it possible to go out to sea in comfort.

For Brenda, Olivia, and Zara at Book Brilliance Publishing for their never-ending patience and faith that the book you now hold in your hands would be published after the ideas for it were swimming around in my head, heart and soul for a long time, a really long time! What a great trio to have by my side.

For Mansour Al Dhaheri and the **Swim62 Abu Dhabi** family for welcoming me to the team just three weeks before the big swim! What an honour to be part of the women's swim team and rekindle my love of open water swimming. Mansour's story in Chapter Nine is a classic hero's journey. **For Will Walker:** I loved your 'storming' story and it's great to see hundreds of children and adults benefiting from swim classes with your team.

For Dr. Brian Luke Seaward: When I read your foreword, my eyes welled up with tears and I had goosebumps! That's a good sign. Thank you for being a bright light on the planet, a fabulous friend, spiritual mentor, and nature advocate.

For Dr. Wallace. J Nichols: Your book *Blue Mind* blew my mind and nourished my water-loving soul. Thank you for gifting your words in support of *Uncharted Waters*. I can't wait to read the 10th Anniversary edition of *Blue Mind* being released in 2024.

For Robbyne Plant of White Wolf Journeys. I loved my time connecting with whales and dolphins in Maui and Bimini. Incredible experiences, lifelong memories and a deeper connection to nature and marine life. I look forward to many more journeys with you. The Ultimate Whale Watching Company in Lahaina and the Wild Quest Dolphin Retreat Centre team are the best. See you in Sedona and several other magical places around the globe!

For Keane Wang, whose instrumental piano tracks filled my seaside studio during the writing and edit process. Your album, **Pacific Lull**, was the perfect soundscape and I continue to listen to it whenever I need to open the portal to my creative flow. Consider me a lifelong raving fan!

For Alisha, my gorgeous, talented niece. You are the singer in our family and have blessed this book with an *Uncharted Waters* soundtrack. I look forward to you singing it live at book launch events. Keep sharing your voice with the world.

For all the authors, philosophers and poets whose quotes and poems you will find flowing through the chapters.

For front cover design and branding – the amazing women at Plug: Lucy, Leilani and Marwa.

For the photographers, Gillian Robertson (back cover picture) and **Pranish Pradhan** (author bio picture).

For Natalie Hore and Hala Dahmane, respective Founder and President of Azraq, for creating an incredible organisation focusing on the health of the oceans and marine life. What an honour it is to support your initiatives through book sales and my speaking engagements.

For YOU, the Reader, who has embarked on this journey with me. I trust that *Uncharted Waters* will inspire you to deepen your connection to water and all the amazing lessons it has to offer when we take the time to look closer and dive deeper.

Last but by no means least, thank you **WATER** for giving life to everything.

With Deep Love and Gratitude.

About the Author

JULIE LEWIS IS AN international sought-after speaker, seasoned explorer and bestselling author. She's best known for her trailblazing journey in the world of adventure and self-discovery. After climbing her first mountain in 2002, she set up the Middle East's first female-led expedition company, Mountain High, an organisation dedicated to pushing the boundaries of human potential and fostering a deeper connection to Nature. Her first book, *Moving Mountains: Discover the Mountain In You*, gave readers the courage, confidence and clarity to unlock their highest potential, realise their dreams, and take consistent purposeful action.

Julie's remarkable career has taken her to the far corners of the globe where she has ventured into uncharted waters – both metaphorically and literally. She has trained and led multi-national teams of men and women on over 70 expeditions and retreats around the globe, including the Arctic and Antarctica, all in the relentless pursuit of uncovering the hidden depths and potential of the human spirit.

With a compelling storytelling ability and an unwavering commitment to empowering others, Julie has inspired countless individuals to embark on their own transformative inner and outer journeys. As a professional speaker, her thought-provoking narratives positively change the way people think, act and feel.

Julie is a regular podcast, radio and TV guest, and TEDx and Million Dollar Round Table speaker. She has delivered keynotes and masterclasses around the globe.

Julie is a beacon of inspiration for those seeking to break free from the confines of comfort and explore the vast oceans of possibilities. Her work resonates with anyone who yearns to uncover their hidden depths and navigate the uncharted waters of life.

In her latest book, *Uncharted Waters: Discover Your Hidden Depths*, Julie invites readers to connect more deeply to water as an element for self-reflection and personal growth.

To engage Julie as a visiting author, guest speaker, or retreat and expeditions leader, take the plunge and reach her through her website: www.julie-lewis.com

Julie Lewis

SPEAKER. EXPLORER. AUTHOR

CONNECT WITH JULIE

www.julie-lewis.com

www.linkedin.com/in/julielewis4/

Instagram: @juliemileslewis

www.facebook.com/julie.lewis.98892/

YouTube: @julielewis9722

For bulk book orders contact:
admin@bookbrilliancepublishing.com